# CASA

# YUCATAN

# CASA YUCATAN

KAREN WITYNSKI & JOE P. CARR

PHOTOGRAPHY BY KAREN WITYNSKI

Gibbs Smith, Publisher
Salt Lake City

**To our families with love and gratitude–Judith M. Simpson, Amy Witynski Holmes, Mara Witynski, Jenny Witynski and Joe P. Carr, Sr., Joe Carr III, Michael Carr.**

First Paperback Edition

10 09 08 07 06   5 4 3 2 1

Text © 2002 by Karen Witynski and Joe P. Carr
Photographs © 2002 by Karen F. Witynski except the following: pg xxvii, pg 89 and pg 188, portrait by James Ray Spahn.

Published by
Gibbs Smith, Publisher
P.O. Box 667
Layton, UT 84041

Orders (1-800) 748-5439
www.gibbs-smith.com

Designed by CN Design
Printed and bound in China

Library of Congress Cataloging-in-Publication Data

Witynski, Karen, 1960-
Casa Yucatán / Karen Witynski and Joe P. Carr.— 1st ed.
p. cm.
ISBN 1-58685-033-4 (hb); 1-4236-0106-8 (pbk)
1. Architecture, Domestic—Mexico—Yucatán Peninsula. 2. Architecture—Mexico—Yucatán Peninsula—20th century. I. Carr, Joe P., 1942-  II. Title.
NA7245.Y83 W58 2002
728.097265—dc21

2002003398

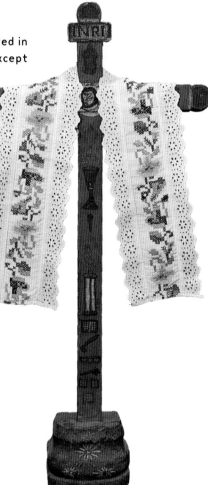

**COVER:** Celebrating color, texture and an artful blend of old and new, this restored Izamal courtyard highlights antique hacienda iron rail tracks as sculpture. Casa de los Artistas, restored by Salvador Reyes Ríos and Josefina Larraín.

**HALF TITLE PAGE:** A vibrant wall fountain at Casa del Panadero features ceramic tiles and a *kancab* finish.

**TITLE PAGE, LEFT:** Framed by elegant arches, the picturesque *portal* at Hacienda Santa Rosa features wall stencils re-created from original patterns found during restoration. Right: Stencil from Hotel Medio Mundo.

**COPYRIGHT PAGE:** Old hand-painted Mayan cross, collection of Joe P. Carr and Karen Witynski.

**CONTENTS:** Hacienda Uayamón's masterful restoration melds modern elegance with the estate's rich history.

**MONTAGE PAGE xvii:** Guadalupe, collection of Ann Bahan. MONTAGE PAGE 53, BOTTOM LEFT: Quinta Faller.

**BACK COVER:** A copper chandelier graces the art-filled sala at Hacienda La Pinka.

# ACKNOWLEDGMENTS

Many dear people contributed generously to this book, sharing their creativity, support and enthusiasm. We are grateful first to our friends in the Yucatán, the homeowners, architects, designers, artists and craftsmen who have shared their knowledge and spirited hospitality over the years. Their tremendous talent and innovation were the inspiration for this volume.

A heartfelt thanks to the people who were an integral part of shaping this book. First, to my sister Amy Witynski Holmes for her brilliant assistance in editing the manuscript. Her writing talent and dedication made the word journey a joyful adventure. We thank our friend and art director Christine Nasser, for her masterful talent and dedication to beauty; our agent Betsy Amster, for her friendship and continued support; and the Gibbs Smith team, including editors Madge Baird and Monica Weeks, for their special support.

We acknowledge with gratitude the assistance of the Government of the State of Yucatán, the Governor, Mr. Patricio Patrón Laviada, and the Secretary of Tourism, Mrs. Carolina Cárdenas Sosa. Their special contribution to our research was invaluable.

We are particularly grateful to our dear friends and colleagues, Salvador Reyes Ríos and Josefina Larraín who generously shared their knowledge and gave freely of their time, hearts, and resources for this project. Their helpful advice and distinctive style were an inspiration every step of the way. Additional thanks to Salvador for writing the foreword and assisting with the manuscript.

We wish to express our deep gratitude to the many people who contributed their valuable efforts to this book: Alvaro Ponce, who showed us the beauty of Yucatán's contemporary homes and inspired us with his talent; Sean Hale, for his research assistance and translations; Miguel Faller, who shared his vast knowledge and helpful leads; Nina Long, who aided us with special contacts and locations; Jen Lytle, who inspired us with her great knowledge of old colonial homes; Francisco Faller and Ann Walström de Faller, for their warm hospitality and assistance with the manuscript.

We would also like to thank the following people who hospitably opened their homes and haciendas to us: Cándida Fernández and Eduardo Calderón, Aurise and Wayne Trotter, Jorge Trava, Jorge and Maricela Seijo, Miguel and Carmen Faller, Bob and Carol Gow, Luis and Laura de Yturbe, Alvaro and Rebecca Ponce, Emilio and Lida Sansores, Alejandro Patrón, Bill Morrow, Cristina Baker and Jorge Ruz, Nicole Samaha and Nelson Laprebendere, Pablo de Costa, Erick Rubio Barthell, John and Dorianne Venator, Ray and Emma Berst, Jim and Ellen Fields, Alberto Salum Abdala, Dr. Hernán Patrón Vales, Lic. Leanardo Silveira Cuevas, Ana Rosa Flores de Gaber and Beatriz Flores. Although they wish to remain anonymous, we extend our thanks to the Mérida homeowners who warmly welcomed us into their homes.

Additional thanks to the following pioneers who lent valuable support: Roberto Hernández and Claudia Madrazo, Luis Bosoms Creixell and Marilu Hernández. Our gratitude to the associates and staff of "The Haciendas," Starwood Hotels and Resorts, Herman Reeling Brouwer, Veronique Timsonet, Karsten Lemke and Marie Anne Zaldua, as well as Guiner Cocom Mena, Marco Antonio May Chin, Jorge Sanchez Lopez, Pablo Estrella, Manuel Ortiz Ake, Luciano Leonor, Gilberto Chin and Jorge Dzima Moreno.

We would like to pay special tribute to friends and associates who have shared their time and knowledge: Andres Solis, Eduardo Cardenás, Roberto Cardenás, Carlos Millet, Michel Antochiw, Juan Carlos Faller, William Ramírez, Rene Gamboa Leon, Carlos Ricalde Medina, Gabriel Konzevik, Alejandro Chimal and Ruben Ojeda. A special note of appreciation to Ana Argáez for her valuable location suggestions, and to Javier Antonio Lizama Chan for his great knowledge of the Yucatán region and expert help as photo assistant.

A special thanks to those who gave insightful advice and help, among them Luis Torre Peraza, Emilio de los Rios ibarra, Mayte Weitzman, Juan Garcia, Anita Carrillo, Josefina Villanueva, Abraham Feralta, Teo Mun Chavez, Colidio Pol Balam, Marty Baird, Ruy Camino, Elsie and Pastor Camino, Maricela Castro, Jorge Bracamonte Leon, Tomas Pacheco Basulto, Mitch Jay Keenan, Enrique Dominguez, Domingo Rodriguez Semerena.

Many thanks to our friends at La Misión de Fray Diego: Luis Florencia, Jorge Durán, Joel Ríos, Cuxtali-Kú Cetina, Luis Carbonell, Ermilio Ojeda, Rubén Cantillo, Jorge Contreras, Gaspar Chan, Jacinto Narvaez, Fátima Gómez, Noemi García, Gerardo Canto, Manuel Castellanos, Humberto Gutiérrez and Raul Pérez.

Finally, our deep appreciation to our families for their constant support, my mother Judith M. Simpson and sisters Amy Witynski Holmes, Mara Witynski and Jenny Witynski. A special thanks to Marion Holmes and Joe P. Carr Sr. A special tribute to my late father, Stanley S. Witynski, who encouraged our vision for book writing years ago.

**We would like to acknowledge Aeromexico for their support with air transportation during our research trips to Mexico.**

**Special thanks to La Misión de Fray Diego for providing us with wonderful accommodations and impeccable service while on location in Mérida.**

# CONTENTS

# FOREWORD

The Yucatán Peninsula's Mexican states—Yucatán, Quintana Roo and northern Campeche—are often considered another country inside the country. Once independent from Mexico, the Yucatán is historically called the "Brother Republic" by its natives. In itself, the peninsula represents an important piece of Mexico's mosaic of multilayered landscapes, weathers and cultures. In a land of virtually no surface rivers or lakes, underground water resources were the fundamental point of origin for human settlements until the twentieth century. These *cenotes* are not only unique Yucatán landmarks but also sacred places of the old Maya civilization. Throughout the north and central regions, low and mid-height jungle is the typical landscape. A flat limestone shelf comprises the surface, a condition resulting in plenty of exposed rock and only a thin layer of soil. Historically, Yucatán topography allows for limited agriculture and has given rise to cattle raising and the harvesting of honey and *henequén* (sisal), staples of the region's economic activity.   The realities of landscape in the Brother Republic have marked the Yucatán with distinctive cultural expressions. As part of these expressions, architecture synthesizes and reflects the imaginations, aspirations and admiration from the people of this land through time: from the earliest Maya to the mixture of both Maya and Spanish mother cultures, and most recently from north and central Mexico, as expressed in the Colonial, Porfiriato and later Mexican Contemporary periods. Architecture in this region has reached what some authorities call the renaissance, or cultural renovation, period, in large part a result of North American influence and late-twentieth-century economic globalization. As an architect, I had been working until 1996 in Mexico City—a metropolis where I was born, raised and educated—primarily in the design of modern residential homes and public buildings. My intrigue with central Mexico's sixteenth-century convents as well as sugar and cattle haciendas led me to further research colonial architecture as a design professor of Metropolitan University, where I also studied for a master's degree in restoration. In 1996, Luis Bosoms Creixell, director and architect of Grupo Plan, invited me to the Yucatán to head up the restoration and architectural projects for a number of nineteenth- and twentieth-century sisal haciendas that were to be adapted as small luxury hotels. It was not a difficult choice to move to the Yucatán, as the project offered a great challenge in architectural analysis and creativity. This part of Mexico was surprisingly different from what I had seen in the rest of the country. The region is densely populated with an endless number of architecturally rich villages, churches and chapels, plazas and traditional Mayan homes, always exhibiting very creative variations on the principal architectural styles according to epoch. Distinct local elements such as stone, palm roofs and lime-stucco finishes are included in numerous designs. Traveling through the vast Yucatán landscape via *sascab* trails (original Maya roads), I was fascinated to always find a big surprise at the end: a village or hacienda, with a single church, chimney or market, all surrounded by the Maya peacefulness and welcoming manner. As associate architect of Grupo Plan, I was involved from 1996 to 2000 in the renovation of six old haciendas. Working with a multidisciplinary team of local and foreign design professionals, contractors and masons proved a valuable experience in studying and recovering buildings, spaces and traditional construction techniques—all the while re-creating others and discovering new ones. In addition to restoring buildings, the project also restored part of the soul of its surrounding villages. Many local masons employed in construction later became waiters, gardeners or maintenance employees when the building work was finished and the hotels opened.  These vital communities, many born and sustained by the hacienda's presence decades ago, are now repeating a life cycle that originated with the earliest haciendas. Thanks to government, private individuals and various institutions, the Yucatán face has changed dramatically in the last decade, creating greater access to the region's historic and cultural richness. This land is not only the gate of the Maya world, but the site of notable colonial architectural settlements like Izamal and Yaxcaba, and close to four hundred haciendas from the Colonial and Porfiriato periods. With a singular architecture of strong character, built with a deep consciousness of climate, haciendas today have become not just subjects of recent renovation but also travel destinations in themselves, just as Maya archeological sites have always been. With their important knowledge of Mexico's distinctive design, Karen Witynski and Joe P. Carr have chosen to focus their attention on the Yucatán, especially its colonial architectural heritage. This book not only represents a new testimony of their passionate interest, but a valuable, never-before-published catalogue of architectural elements—clearly classified by historical periods—that exposes the distinctive architectural expressions that define part of Yucatán's multilayered identity. Karen and Joe, in association with their partners, the Sterns, found their own piece of Yucatán art and history at Hacienda Petac. Its restoration is an additional contribution to Yucatán's cultural renovation. This spontaneous movement is extending to Mérida downtown neighborhoods and a number of extraordinary hundred-year-old houses that are being rescued and renovated as homes. Along with my partner Josefina Larraín, the authors of this book, and many notable individuals and institutions, we are together promoting the continuity of this movement. *Casa Yucatán* is an invitation to join us.

—**Salvador Reyes Ríos**

Hacienda Santa Rosa's *casa principal* features a series of elegant arches and a decorative frieze.
OPPOSITE: A colonial window shows off thick stone walls.

THE DISTINCTIVE LANDSCAPE OF THE YUCATAN PENINSULA POSSESSES A UNIQUE NATURAL BEAUTY WHERE LIMESTONE PLATEAUS, TROPICAL JUNGLES AND SUBTERRANEAN RIVERS AND CAVES ARE THE SETTING OF TWO MAGNIFICENT CULTURES.

# INTRODUCTION

**Spanning from city to countryside to coast**, the Yucatán boasts traditional Maya villages amidst ancient archaeological ruins, sprawling haciendas, solitary beaches, bustling markets and old colonial towns with shady plazas that pair elegant city homes with sixteenth- and seventeenth-century churches. In its mysterious mix of Maya temples and Spanish Colonial convents, the region is rich with pre-Hispanic and colonial architecture.

*Casa Yucatán* came about through our explorations of the intersection of old and new in the architecture and design of Yucatán homes, gardens and haciendas. In part an extension of our previous book—*The New Hacienda*—and partly a new discovery of colonial and contemporary homes, this volume expresses the captivating blend of cultures and influences we found in the peninsula's three states of Yucatán, Campeche and Quintana Roo. The homes we reveal express the grandeur of the Yucatán's early Maya and colonial eras in confluence with an emerging, contemporary design style that is distinctively Yucatecan.

Our research for *The New Hacienda*—which heralded the beginnings of this hacienda revival—introduced us to the Yucatán's innovative design community and allowed us to witness the region's tremendous growth, local resources and artistic ingenuity. Many restored haciendas have risen out of the Yucatán's rich terrain in recent years, adding a dimension of glamour to the rural geography with their doors newly opened as hacienda resorts. Today, their rustic charm blends with European inheritances: colorfully patterned cement floor tiles, stenciled walls and colonial antiques. These "jewels in the jungle" have garnered acclaim for their preservation pioneers and have attracted a slew of international travelers savvy to the Yucatán's growing profile via travel magazines.

During our work for *The New Hacienda*, it became evident to us that this remarkable renaissance was extending beyond the rural landscape into the colonial cities: homes and entire neighborhoods in Mérida, Izamal, Valladolid and Campeche were undergoing fascinating renovations and attracting homeowners from the U.S., Canada, Europe and other parts of Mexico. As we collected countless photos of revivals for *The New Hacienda*, we were privileged to glimpse incredible design innovations taking place in grand-scale city homes, contemporary houses and coastal retreats. Our passion for the region re-sparked, we set off to meet more of the individuals responsible for reawakening the hacienda style in new constructions, and who have incorporated Mexican Colonial design elements into modern homes. This new generation of architects, designers, craftsmen and artists was more than generous in sharing their vision and knowledge with us. Others, including hacienda owner Miguel Faller, greatly enriched our pilgrimages by leading us to locations of lesser-known colonial treasures.

With the completion of *The New Hacienda*, we vowed to make regular visits to the Yucatán, to continue exploring the region's elusive mix of history, gracious open-air living and design details refined by centuries of experimentation. Our treks through the numerous Maya villages that dot the peninsula led us to sights and experiences that set the groundwork for this, the fifth book in our Mexican Design series. New luxe Maya *casitas*, Mexican contemporary homes sited amidst myriad interior courtyards and water features,

A dramatic arch and elegant tiles echo the noble past of Hacienda Uayamón in Campeche.

and old Porfiriato-era homes confirmed to us the presence of a uniquely Yucatecan design style we became passionate about sharing.

We were endeared to the warmth and friendliness of the Yucatecan people, and delighted in watching artisans at work weaving hammocks, shaping pottery and masterfully embroidering *huipiles* (women's blouses). In handwork and architecture, ancient history was close at hand: it was astounding to visit a colonial-era home in Izamal whose courtyard's west side was enclosed by a massive stone wall of a sixth-century pyramid. At a colonial estate south of Mérida, we stumbled upon a vine-shrouded Maya observatory and felt the sky's lure as we climbed its narrow steps to look over roof and tree tops. We were exhilarated in a descent on foot into a sacred *cenote* (underground well) and became witness to its watery labyrinths and pre-Hispanic glyphs engraved in limestone walls. A later trip to a hacienda estate brought our water experience aboveground, this time in a warm hacienda pool built, ironically, around the old columns of a never-completed ice factory.

Uxmal's ancient ruins are a testament to the Mayans' masterful stone carving.

OPPOSITE: An iguana finds quiet sanctuary in the stone ruins of Uxmal, Yucatán.

The new homes we visited took their design cues from the rich textures of Yucatecan stone and old-world methods of painting with mineral pigments. The Mayans' masterful legacies—carved stone and stucco ornaments, a ceremonial homage to color and water—were everywhere in evidence. We were smitten with colorful walls of sun-drenched red, burnt ocher and blue that brought subtle traditional details to life: mesmerizing stone-chinked surface patterns and raised-stucco designs. Throughout the region, we followed an intriguing trail of textures, from stone-carved door surrounds to columns embedded with seashells from the coast. Textural details in the peninsula's seaside homes—and in beach houses extending to Quintana Roo's Mayan Riviera—were a distillation of natural elements including pebble-mosaic floors and woven-fiber furnishings.

We eventually focused our travels in Mérida, an inviting cosmopolitan city built in 1542 on top of the ancient Maya city T'ho. We returned there for weeks at a time, relishing in the splendor of the Yucatán capital's colonial architectural heritage and nineteenth-century French influences. (In many areas of culture and design, European influence was prominent in this region of the peninsula, which kept closer ties with Europe than with the rest of Mexico due to its geographical isolation and independent spirit.) Not least, we delighted in the cultural expressions in traditional music and dance found in shady plazas, weekly outdoor orchestral concerts and sidewalk art and craft fairs. Clip-clopping via *calesa* (horse-drawn carriage) down tree-lined boulevards modeled after the Champs-Elysées, we viewed *henequén*-era mansions ornamented with elegant architectural details: intricate ironwork, pilastered façades, and parapets. As we explored old neighborhoods undergoing renovation, we fueled ourselves via regular stops at Cuban cafes and local fruit markets.

Somewhere in the midst of our early days of climbing around hacienda ruins to document original architectural details, a desire to rescue and preserve a hacienda property of our own was kindled. We were excited to coalesce our desire to restore a colonial property with the many talents and know-how of the design pioneers we were meeting in the Yucatán. As we learned more about these individuals' devotion and commitment to honoring prehistoric and colonial legacies in their interpretations of contemporary living spaces, our dream of renovating a hacienda for both personal and public posterity was fueled. The two-year design adventure with Hacienda Petac is revealed in our Haciendas chapter.

Intrigued by Campeche's downtown architecture, we toured Casa Seis and Casa del Teniente del Rey and marveled at their classic façades,

Antique *santos* and treasured elements are crowned by decorative iron. Alberto's Continental Patio.

OPPOSITE: Colonial antiques and *santos* decorate Hacienda Poxilá's elegant library.

An impressive collection of ancient Maya artifacts are displayed at Hacienda Yaxcopoil.

OPPOSITE: A three-tiered copper chandelier graces the art-filled *sala* at Hacienda La Pinka.

inner courtyards, tile patterns and wall stencils. Walking through restored neighborhoods coated in tangerine and pistachio hues, we stepped back further in time to view impressive pre-Hispanic stone *stele* (stone columns decorated with Maya hieroglyphs) and carved lintels at the Museum of the Stele. From the walled tower of San Miguel Fort, the waters of Yucatán's once-busiest port appeared fairly quiet. Centuries earlier, the port of Campeche bustled with European ships loaded with prized logwood sought for its red dye.

From our initial trips to the Yucatán, we were enamored with the first haciendas converted to restaurants, hotels and museums, including Hacienda Teya, Hacienda Chichén, Hacienda Yax-copoil, Hacienda Katanchel and the first three Grupo Plan haciendas: Temozón, Santa Rosa and San José Cholul. With their vision for the Grupo Plan projects, Roberto Hernández and his director and architect of the projects, Luis Bosoms Creixell, have been key leaders in the region. Most recently, their efforts have expanded to include colonial city buildings, the Phoenix Maya project and more haciendas: Hacienda Uayamón, Hacienda Chichi de los Lagos and Hacienda Ochil, which houses a *henequén* museum, artisan workshops and open-air restaurant. The preservation work by the Grupo Plan team reveals innovative

**A peaceful plant-filled courtyard is framed by graceful stone arches at Casa Gaber Flores.**

**OPPOSITE: Early hand-painted murals encircle old hammock hooks and decorate walls at Casa Gaber Flores.**

colonial techniques and has inspired many in their creative, adaptive reuse. Throughout our research, architect Salvador Reyes Ríos and designer Josefina Larraín generously shared their knowledge of Yucatán design, as did many talented restoration and history experts, including Francisco Faller, author Michel Antochiw, and architect Alvaro Ponce.

This vital and pioneering work of Yucatán's preservationists, architects, artists, restoration experts and homeowners is keeping alive the Yucatán's rich and varied physical history. The rescue and restoration efforts that started with churches, convents and rural haciendas now envelop colonial city buildings and are serving as catalysts for more extensive private and public revivification projects. In addition to benefiting local Maya communities with sources of work, many rural restoration projects have renewed local knowledge of ancient building methods.

A beautifully carved cabinet and old ceramic pot rest in a corner of the Casa Seis kitchen in Campeche.
OPPOSITE: An old-world kitchen at Casa Seis features a tiled counter, tall ceilings and a hanging basket.

An iron candelabra, Maya crosses and hand-painted walls adorn the chapel at Hacienda San José Cholul.

As designers and gallery owners, we have been on a continuous quest to witness and document the people, elements and places steering contemporary design movements that honor the history and cultures throughout Mexico. Through this volume, we feel privileged to be able to document and present the richness and wonder of Yucatecan design and the expertise of those helping to create it.

As witnesses to the physical and ethereal treasures of this peninsula, we share the feelings for the Yucatán best described by artist Claudia Madrazo: "Visiting the Maya world is like discovering a paradise, a place lost in time. The smiles . . . the wisdom in the conversation . . . and a tradition hidden in their patios. There is something mysterious and true, something magical. It is a place that makes souls vibrate."

A Yucatecan woman gazes through the graceful doors of the Izamal church. Photograph by Carlos Stern.

A courtyard wall, restored by Salvador Reyes Ríos, features rich textures: *rajueleado* and *kancab*.

OPPOSITE: A *henequén* stalk rests against a richly textured wall finished with *kancab*.

EACH REGION THROUGHOUT MEXICO'S MAYA WORLD IS CHARACTERIZED BY A DISTINCTIVE VOCABULARY OF DESIGN TEXTURES THAT EMANATE FROM GEOGRAPHICAL LOCATION, ABUNDANT NATURAL RESOURCES AND CULTURAL HISTORY.

# DESIGN TEXTURES

**In the Yucatán**, the abundance of limestone, dearth of soil and tropical climate define its textural vocabulary. In the nearby state of Chiapas, a cooler climate and the abundance of rich soil and wood define its design details. Today, innovative designers and architects are making use of indigenous materials and methods to underscore the spirit of the rich Yucatecan past. On walls, floors and other surfaces, handcrafted techniques

in stone, stucco, paint, tile, wood, clay and fiber add unique texture that infuses depth and time-honored character to Yucatán interiors, garden walls and outdoor living spaces.

Throughout Yucatán homes and haciendas, textural details create unique statements: tropical hardwood doors are studded with old iron *chapetones* (large nail heads) and flanked with carved-stone surrounds to add special definition to entrances. Interior courtyard walls feature thousands of hand-placed chinked stones to create dramatic backdrops for sculpture and artwork. Aged walls with colonial-patterned *cenefas* (stencils) display an elegantly simple solution to decoration. Colorful kitchens are a blend of tile texture, in floors patterned with concrete tiles and counters of hand-painted ceramic tiles. For contrast, cement tiles are surrounded by a polished cement border.

Pre-Hispanic and Spanish Colonial influences upon stonework yield an abundance of textural markings that bear evidence of the human hand. Ranging from the creamy whites of *macedonia* and fossilized-shell surfaces of *conchuela* and *coquina*, to the sunset orange and red hues of Ticul stone, the region boasts a rich legacy of stone textures used as much to decoratively define as to functionally support.

For centuries, the Mayans adeptly utilized stone and the resources of earth, mineral pigments, plants and trees for architectural decoration and utility. From ornately carved limestone reliefs, intricate stucco embellishments, and colorful murals that remain vibrant after centuries, the Maya culture made masterful use of its environment to reveal a deep spirituality and devotion to the natural world.

In addition to architectural elements and fountains, stone is shaped into numerous objects, including table bases, planters, crosses and Maya figures. Also prevalent are hand-carved sinks, even those that mimic the shapes of Maya water troughs. At Hacienda Temozón, rescued stone columns provide the base for carved *macedonia* sinks in an elegant bathroom floored in a grid of black marble and white concrete.

**A circular, stone-chinking pattern enlivens this elegant Mérida home built by Francisco J. Faller Manazanilla.**

Baptismal fonts are an example of a colonial relic reinspired for use as garden vessels for aquatic plants.

Stone plays an important accent role when it is creatively positioned. At the base of a *nicho* or embedded in old walls to protrude beyond the wall plane, the placement of stone creates textural interest by throwing shadows that break up large wall surfaces. As decorative embellishment upon colorful concrete floors, lines of small chinked stones provide unique border lines to an overall floor pattern. Trails of small chinked stones are seen encircling larger stones in myriad pathways. In coastal areas, lime-stuccoed stone columns are sometimes embedded with tiny seashells.

Both beauty and utility are brought to the surface in walls that trace and express the regional traditions of decorative stone use. One of the most mesmerizing stone design methods, *rajueleado* is traditionally utilized in an exterior wall, using repetition of stone chinks to punctuate a stuccoed wall in a variety of patterns. *Rajueleado* is both decorative and functional, as it creates a dramatic wall texture while also working to consolidate and prevent cracks in the stucco.

A smooth *macedonia* column and chinked limestone wall.

OPPOSITE: A sculpture by Carlos Terres hangs on a *rajueleado* Ticul stone wall designed by Alvaro Ponce.

Another popular use of chinked stone is seen in floor-to-ceiling walls comprised completely of small stones "chinked" from larger stones, each one hand-cut and uniquely formed. Traditional façades in the southern state of Yucatán near Ticul and also into Campeche are made of fully chinked walls. These texturally rich, intricate walls are favored by architect Alvaro Ponce, who uses them in contemporary Mexican interiors. For indigenous splashes of color and pattern, Ponce employs the region's rich orange Ticul stone and white limestone for these chinked walls both inside and out.

**An inviting stairwell blends wrought iron, ceramic tiles and cheerfully painted walls at Hotel Medio Mundo.**

Hand-carved *macedonia* sinks rest atop rescued columns in the elegant bathroom suite at Hacienda Temozón.

Masterful Maya stone carving is revealed at the ancient ruins of Uxmal, Yucatán.

OPPOSITE, TOP: An old carved-stone shell is prominently displayed in a wall nicho at Hacienda Xixim.

RIGHT: A simple carved-stone pattern adds decorative interest to a door surround.

Similar effects are evoked by the use of *conchuela* in stone walls. A type of coastal stone featuring a fossilized surface, *conchuela* yields intriguing textures when bathed in direct sunlight or through overhead skylights, both being means of dramatizing the intricate imprints of small shells. This effect is beautifully mastered in the Trotter home, designed by architect Javier Muñoz. The twenty-foot *conchuela* stone wall faces the dining area, providing a natural work of art for the open-air living space. *Conchuela*'s textural surface also provides inspiration for Yucatán designer Carlos Millet, who uses the

surface as a unique backdrop for decorative painted scenes. Well known for his large-scale wall murals, Millet also adds decorative interest and texture to contemporary homes with his artistic designs that are hand-painted along walls, door wells and ceilings.

The Yucatán's regional vegetation metamorphoses into art and architecture in a variety of ways: palm fronds, grasses and vines lashed together for thatched roofs and fashioned into hats, baskets and folk art. *Anikab,* a strong vine found in the southern regions of the Yucatán, is ingeniously woven into large bas-

kets, furniture and the occasional door for traditional Maya homes. *Henequén* fiber, the source of Yucatán's great wealth in the region's *oro verde* (green gold) era of the late nineteenth- to early twentieth-century, has found multiple uses in addition to its export for rope and twine. Renowned for its strength and natural color, *henequén* is creatively woven into hammocks, baskets, window shades and floor coverings. New innovations with *henequén* also include woven fan-pulls and cabinet handles. Additionally, artisans are crafting bags and embellishing gourds.

Elegant wall stencils at Hacienda Santa Rosa were re-created from original patterns.

OPPOSITE: A worn hammock hook plays host to a collection of Mexican textile bags.

A colorful kitchen boldly blends textures at Casa Reyes-Larraín: old floor tiles are surrounded by a polished cement frame and ceramic tiles front the counter.

Contemporary artists are also finding inspiration in this indigenous fiber as they incorporate it into a variety of mediums. Artist Joan Duran's *henequén* artworks include photographic images and installations with live baby plants. His works related to *henequén* have been shown in Mérida, Mexico City, Salt Lake City and Belize City. The 1999 e-ki exhibition at Mérida's Museo Palacio Cantón was totally conceived around *henequén* and included paintings, lightboxes, photographs and live installations.

**At Casa Reyes-Larraín, a mahogany door, Spanish tile and cement floor tiles combine for a rich statement.**

*Henequén*, naturally colored soils and indigenous plant material found in Mexico are sources of inspiration for visual artist Marty Baird. Revealing local colors, patterns and textures, Baird's mixed-media works are historical portraits of ruins, haciendas and colonial buildings whose physical qualities contribute to the paintings' narrative meaning. Just as the stories of these ancient structures are embedded in their walls, the layers and textures in Baird's paintings document change and reveal much about these colonial places. In addition to solo and group exhibitions in Mexico, Europe, Brazil and the U.S., Baird shares her experimental approach to working with natural pigments through lectures and workshops throughout the U.S. and Mexico.

A hammock made from Sanseviera fiber, commonly called *lengua de vaca*.

OPPOSITE: Yucatán stone wall details; embroidered Maya textile from San Jolobil Workshop in San Cristobal Las Casas; *henequén* market bag.

The weathered textures of an arcaded exterior at Hacienda Uayamón, Campeche.

Yucatán's pre-Hispanic communities utilized a variety of natural resources for the creation of unique paint finishes and sealants. Today, traditional earthen pigments and *cal* (lime-based paint) continue to be favored for their natural finishes and ability to breathe and wear well on limestone buildings. Innovative architects have reintroduced these age-old methods that yield special colors and textures for walls, *bancos* (built-in benches) and exterior surfaces.

*Hacienda Story* by Marty Baird incorporates local natural materials in its surface texture.

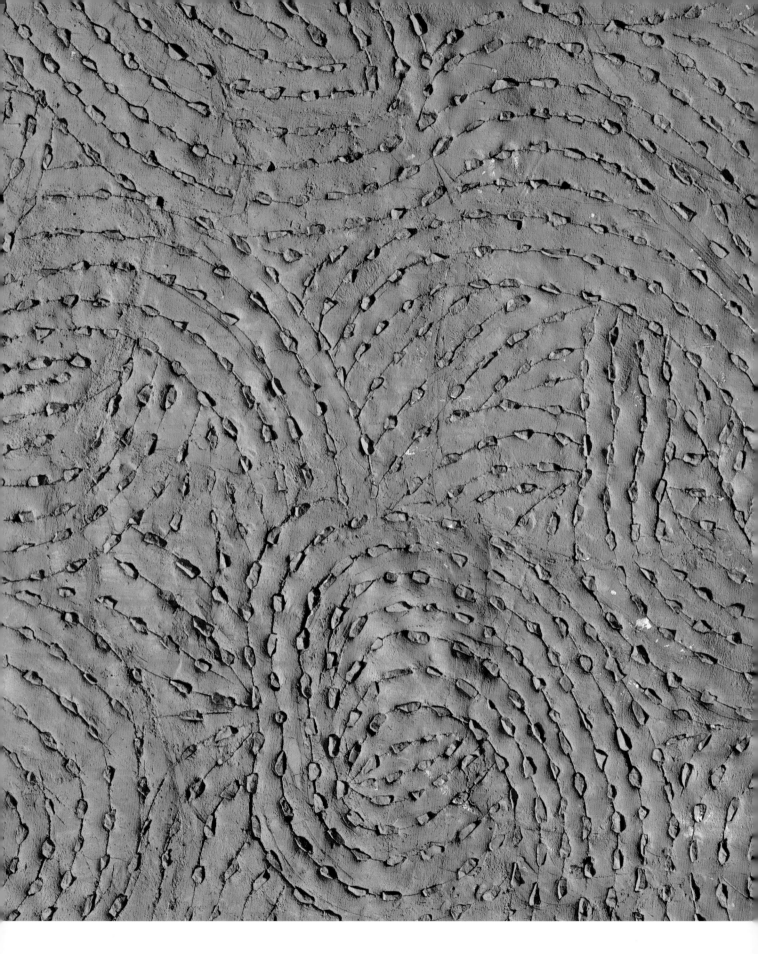

A mesmerizing example of hand-placed stone chinking on an exterior wall.

OPPOSITE: A richly textured exterior wall at Hacienda San José Cholul's Maya *casita*.

*Kancab*, a deep red earth obtained in southern Yucatán, and *sascab*, a white earth, are surfacing with captivating results on many present building projects. Plant-based resins, including *chukum* and *pixoy*, are also being re-introduced in new applications by architect Salvador Reyes Ríos. Originally created by the Mayans to seal water cisterns, the natural-hued *chukum* finish is a tree resin that creates a smooth finish impermeable to water and is beautifully translucent. *Pixoy* resin is used similarly to *chukum*, though *pixoy* can be mixed with color pigments to bring a shiny texture to surfaces. Both resins are presently used today on pools and Jacuzzis.

Stone-paved corridors with beamed ceilings surround the courtyard at the Museum of Secular Art, Conkal.

OPPOSITE: A simple wall *nicho* holds a stone-carved cross in Izamal.

THE STONE RESOURCES OF THE YUCATAN'S VAST LIMESTONE PLATEAU YIELD THE
MOST INFLUENCE IN THE REGION'S DESIGN AND ARCHITECTURE AS EVIDENCED IN
THE REMARKABLE TEMPLES AND VAST CITIES THE ANCIENT MAYA SKILLFULLY CARVED
FROM LIMESTONE AND DECORATED WITH LIME STUCCO AND COLORFUL PIGMENTS.

# ARCHITECTURAL ELEMENTS

**As the principal construction material**, stone was also shaped and carved in infinite ways for architectural embellishment. *Marcos*, or stone surrounds carved in bas-relief, create decorative outlines for doorways and windows. Massive stone columns support arcaded *portales*, and decorative merlons adorn the tops of elegant roofs. Underfoot, large stone pavers encircle courtyard wells and decoratively outline lily ponds and fountains.

On walls, the juxtaposition of stones is a vibrant testament to the region's rich resources: the deep orange and red hues of Ticul stone are a sunrise of color alongside the cream-white of *macedonia* and the fossilized surfaces of *conchuela* and *coquina*.

The use of tropical hardwoods is also age-old, employed by pre-Hispanic cultures mainly for massive roof beams and lintels. In his early-nineteenth-century observation of the interior of El

Castillo of Chichén Itzá, American explorer John Lloyd Stephens testifies to this use and also to the predominance of carved ornamentation: "Single doorways face the east, south, and west having massive lintels of *sapote* wood, covered with elaborate carvings and the stone jambs are ornamented with figures."

This centuries-old Maya style of ornamentation has influenced architects and designers from the colonial period to the present day. In addition to wood being crafted into ceiling beams, it is widely used in a variety of door styles. Traditional mineral paints that adorn modern-day walls in rich colors, and old-world stencils that decorate *nichos* and wainscoting are other decorative means that continue centuries-old techniques in modern-day homes.

## EARLY CHARACTERISTICS

In response to the tropical climate, stone buildings were constructed with thick walls, high ceilings and covered *portales* (porches). In the colonial period, lofty ceilings featured exposed round wood beams called *rollizos* before square beams became prevalent in the later Porfiriato period (1880–1910). Colonial-epoch dwellings

usually featured *rollizos* with wooden *mensulas* (corbels) to support one main longitudinal *viga madrina* (beam). During the Porfiriato period, ceilings were comprised of many individual beams (either wood or iron) and supported by smaller *mensulas*.

Supporting arcaded *portales*, stone columns were carved both round and square, and those constructed in the colonial era did not often reach beyond eight feet. The earliest doors and windows were also shorter in height than those of the Porfirian period. As the aesthetic of the Porfirian period reveled in large-scale grandeur, the design of doors and windows prior to this time were shorter and less decorated. For colo-

nial ornament, painted decorative outlines were common along the tops of walls and were seen later surrounding doorways. Colonial roof parapets, particularly on haciendas, were often designed with an *espadaña* (bell arch), and decorative friezes and cornices were added during the Porfirian period.

## ENTRANCE ARCHES

Ornate entrance arches, including the *mixtilineo* arch characterized by its Moorish style, are typical of the colonial period's baroque influence. *Pínaculos* (diamond cutouts) and decorative finials adorn this style of hacienda arch. Small

The massive stone entrance arch at Hacienda San José Cholul has a commanding presence.
OPPOSITE: An old carved-stone door surround adds character to this home designed by Alvaro Ponce.

At Hacienda Poxilá, a colorful *capialzado* accents a grilled window and old corbels support an antique trunk.

OPPOSITE: Decorative *capialzados* top windows and doors in a variety of colors and shapes.

pyramidal-shaped details called *almenas* were also common decorative details. More massive and geometrically simple arches are characteristic of the transition between the earliest *henequén* (1860–1880) and Porfiriato (1880–1910) periods. Entrances comprised of a series of square columns as at Hacienda Itzincab and Petectunich are characteristic of the Porfiriato's golden era, or sisal boom.

## DOORS AND WINDOWS

A conical-shaped ornament called a *capialzado* is another prominent, baroque-inspired feature of Yucatán buildings that appears over the exterior head of doors and windows. It is most often painted white to contrast with colorful exterior walls. Inside, the interior head of windows and doors is recessed in a concave shape called *derrame*, which sometimes features the addition of a decorative shell motif.

Although not a heavily forested region, the Yucatán Peninsula does have a variety of tropical woods available, particularly in the southern regions of Quintana Roo and Yucatán State and farther south into Campeche. *Zapote* and *machiche* are two of the strongest indigenous hardwoods. Other hardwoods include *caoba* (mahogany), *tzalam*, *pucté*, *guayacán*, *chacté* and *jabín*. Cedar and heart pine are additionally used.

A traditional Yucatán-style door with a unique window to encourage ventilation, Hacienda Itzincab.

A decorative wooden pediment with cutout designs reduces sun exposure to Hacienda Temozón's *portal*.

Typical door styles include *cañon* doors constructed of simple flat planks, commonly seen on hacienda workshop buildings or storehouses. *Tableros*, or raised-panel doors that featured sophisticated carving, were most often used on important colonial buildings. Other door styles with louvered shutters or *postigos* (small windows) were devised to encourage ventilation. Additional innovations designed to shield *portal* spaces from harsh sun were made with wooden pediments, upon which small cutout designs were added for decorative interest.

The French influence during the Porfiriato period prompted the use of ornate iron window grilles that not only offered protection but also added a decorative feature to colonial homes. Many of the grand mansions built along Mérida's Paseo de Montejo featured intricate ironwork, including railings, grilles and balconies.

## FLOORS

Early floors were stone or lime-based *calcreto* (concrete), often stamp-pressed to simulate various tile patterns. *Calcreto* tiles were used in high traffic areas and labeled "iron tile" for their strength. Red clay tiles were imported from France during the colonial period and used in outdoor patios and covered *portales*. In order to

Golden-hued wainscoting and rich blue doors enhance this spacious bedroom at Hacienda Poxilá.

mark the transition between interior and exterior, door wells contained a linear stone insert that defined the change from indoor to outdoor tiles. Grids of small chinked stones were also used to encircle larger stones in myriad pathways, as seen at Hacienda Temozón. Decorative bands of these "chinked" stones also add graphic interest to colored and polished cement floors. The floors of Yucatán's old homes and colonial haciendas are beautifully decorated with richly patterned cement tiles (*mosaicos de pasta*). Originating in France and Spain, these tiles traveled to the Yucatán on ships that carried them as ballast along with marble and clay roof tiles. As clay

for indigenous tile-making was in short supply in the Yucatán, cement-based tiles were well received and ideally suited for the region's climate and design tastes. Myriad patterns were used within one home.

Rafael R. Quintero, a Yucatán visionary who realized the potential for export to other parts of Mexico and the U.S., imported tile-making technology and machinery from Italy at the turn of the twentieth century. After establishing the first cement-tile factory in Mérida, Quintero expanded the operation over the years to build a successful legacy. His pioneering process continues, in which tiles are formed by a cold press,

using cement, sand, minerals pigments and local limestone. The tile's special brightness and radiance is attributed to the fine Gulf Coast sand used in the tile's top layer. Continuing in operation today, the Mosaicos Traqui factory exports its Astratile through a network of distributors and design showrooms. From modern homes in Florida to hacienda-style ranches in Texas and California, U.S.–based Astratile representative Nina Long has seen the tiles integrated into a variety of architectural environments. Additionally, homeowners are following early traditions of using different tile patterns in each room to create bold statements.

An ornately patterned cement-tile floor at Quinta El Olvido in Mérida.

OPPOSITE: Lofty ceilings and old colonial cement tiles distinguish the grand *sala* of Hacienda Yaxcopoil.

With the rise in old-home renovation and homeowner interest in the salvage of original tiles, creative floor developments have surfaced that give prominence to the intact original tiles often collected during restoration work. Tiles recycled after the removal of old floors (for leveling and the addition of new pipes) are often placed in a floor's center, surrounded by a polished cement border that "frames" the original tiles.

In addition to rough-cut limestone for patios and outdoor spaces, polished stone tile—especially Ticul stone, *conchuela* and *macedonia*—has gained in popularity today. A number of new contemporary homes feature marble floors in inlaid contrasting patterns or in a solid crosscut of travertine called *fiorito*. Architect Eduardo Cárdenas has a penchant for designing dramatic entrance halls in this fashion and utilizes contrasting tones of marble to create the inlaid design's statement.

Carved-stone spheres beautifully anchor a floor fountain in this home by architect Alvaro Ponce.

OPPOSITE: The Ticul stone-tile wall by Alvaro Ponce provides a pleasing backdrop to this interior garden space.

## WALLS

*Cal*, or lime-based paint, is traditionally favored because it bonds well to lime stucco and allows stone walls to breathe. Earthen pigments, including the deep red earth from southern Yucatán State called *kankab*, are mixed with indigenous tree-based resins such as *pixoy* to produce natural finishes that protect and add color to old stone walls. Other resin-based recipes originally used by the Maya have been revived for use as sealants in water receptacles and are discussed on page 85 in the Water Spaces chapter.

Richly decorated with *cenefas* (stencils) that were often inspired by European architectural drawings, colonial walls showed representative images of ornate urns and fleur-de-lis patterns, designs also popular in haciendas and private chapels. Later eras saw an increase in geometric-influenced stencils with repeated bold lines, as well as patterns that appeared as dominant borders above colorful wainscoting.

An original window guard features hand-turned spindles.

OPPOSITE: A colonial hacienda's *portal* features exposed *rollizos*, tile floors and traditional leather *butacas*.

In addition to stencils that utilize one pattern in a stamping process, there has been a revival of hand-painted decorative details, including vine and flower patterns and European-influenced designs. Carlos Millet is one designer well known for his decorative, hand-painted artistry—exhibited on murals, furniture and accessories—that adds a unique decorative element to numerous homes in Mérida as well as contemporary beach homes along the coast. In addition to murals that reflect tranquil seascapes, Millet has also enhanced stone-chinked walls with painted motifs and applied decorative designs to window coverings.

OPPOSITE, TOP: A colonial building is resplendent with original raised-stucco patterns.

OPPOSITE, BOTTOM: Elegant stencils decorate the walls of Casa Seis in Campeche.

Many colonial buildings feature exterior wall surfaces of *rajueleado*, an old method of using *rajuela* (small chinked stones). This technique was devised to consolidate and prevent cracks in the stucco while adding decorative interest. Usually seen as a slash line with a single stone embedded in the center, this chinking method has taken on a variation of patterns and styles. Izamal, east of Mérida, is a colonial city alive with many expressions of *rajueleado* patterns. Exterior walls are finely chinked in infinite variations: circles, diamonds, starburst, or wavy lines. Some *rajueleado* walls depict floral motifs in repetitive patterns. The artistry in wall surfaces is myriad in this region and is widely seen from Valladolid to Campeche.

Another version of *rajueleado* features fully chinked walls comprised completely of hand-cut small stones "chinked" from a larger stone. This technique is characteristic of the region and seen in early homes in southern Yucatán and Campeche.

These traditional façades of fully chinked walls have inspired many of today's architects, including Alvaro Ponce, who features these intricate walls in both interiors and exteriors.

Other exterior wall details included the colonial-era use of lime stucco creatively formed into stucco patterns. In addition to striated lines and geometric forms painted with contrasting colors, more intricate designs were crafted, including the X motif seen on colonial buildings.

The masterful exteriors of churches and convents of the colonial period featured many carved niches that held stone figures of patron saints. Interior *nichos* were home to skillfully carved wooden saints (*santos*) that were painted in intricate detail. Stone or wooden crosses were also featured and continue to stand in *nichos* today. Modern-day *nichos* in homes and gardens often feature the Virgin of Guadalupe and are outlined in hand-painted stencils or lined with stone or ceramic tile.

A picturesque tiled *nicho* adds charm to the luxuriant gardens at Casa Seijo in Mérida.
OPPOSITE: Decoratively outlined windows punctuate stone-chinked walls in Yucatán colonial towns.

## ROOFS

Early roofs of rubble stone and *calcreto* were supported with wooden beams. Iron beams imported from Belgium arrived in the nineteenth century and were widely used throughout haciendas and colonial homes. Also arriving on European ships, French roof tiles (*tejas*) made in Marseille became popular for roofing, particularly for *portales*, a trend that continues in popularity today.

Many of the old iron-beam roofs are also being adapted today for the addition of increased light. By opening up each end of a ceiling with skylights, the modified ceiling floods the room in extra light, which highlights old wall textures and creates the appearance that the roof is floating.

**ABOVE: Hacienda Teya's elegant church features a masterfully chinked exterior.**

**LEFT: Massive buttresses enveloped in vines lend support to the high walls.**

**OPPOSITE: Old French roof tiles enliven the *portal* roof at Hacienda Xcanatún.**

Striped light adds drama to the contemporary pool designed by Javier Muñoz at Casa Trotter Escalante.

OPPOSITE: A Ticul stone spout spills water from an elegant pool wall designed by Alvaro Ponce.

ORIGINATING FROM THE MAYAN WORD DZ'ONOT, MEANING SACRED WELL, CENOTES (SUBTERRANEAN WELLS) WERE THE LIFE-SUSTAINING WATERS OF THE MAYA CULTURE.

# WATER SPACES

**Situated in a rough ring** surrounding the point where a meteor impacted the ocean floor off the north coast of the Yucatán 65 million years ago, the subterranean *cenotes* were indeed viewed by Mayans as gifts from the heavens. These secret underground wells also played a vital role in the Mayans' multilayered vision of the universe. *Cenotes* were viewed as entrances to the underworld where communications with their many

gods—including Chaac, the rain deity—were possible through ritual offerings and sacrifice.

As surface water in the Yucatán is scarce and the dry season lengthy, unique solutions were required for collecting, storing and distributing water, both from these mysterious underground wells and from the rains above. The work of water containment has been one of the principal definers pertaining to the Yucatán's cultural and

architectural history, from pre-Hispanic times through the Spanish Colonial period. In great and sometimes intricate evidence throughout the Yucatán landscape, the elements and design features crafted for this purpose by ancient Mayans and their successors are testaments to the region's lifeblood.

In contemporary homes and colonial restoration projects, new water spaces—both inside and out—pay homage to the Yucatán's devotion to water. Once integral to the efficient collection and distribution of water, stoneworks in the forms of large troughs, storage tanks, aqueduct systems and spouts, as well as colonial-style fountains and decorative reflecting pools, now inspire contemporary architects and designers who incorporate these water spaces as an essential part of Yucatán dwellings.

From the region's natural wells that tap into the water flowing beneath the limestone plateau, to ancient Maya cisterns and the intricate irrigation systems of the hacienda epoch, the cavities and containers of Yucatán's water heritage are redefined today as pools, plunge baths, garden ponds, fountains and flowing water channels. Old *bebederos*, or expansive water troughs built into corrals for watering livestock, are newly filled with water hyacinths as

**Towering over the pool at Hacienda Santa Rosa is the old chimney adjacent to the machine house.**
**OPPOSITE: The ruins of an old ice factory inspired this new dramatic pool at Hacienda Uayamón, Campeche.**

decorative garden features. Former *caños*, or waterspouts, are now activated to spill *agua* for purely aesthetic reasons. Old Maya carved-stone *pilas*, once used as small water troughs, are today seen inside colonial homes, perhaps filled with water lilies as mini water gardens on patios and terraces.

The early Mayans obtained water directly from the *cenotes* via wells that were created by making holes in the lime-stone surface. As rain-water filtered through the soft, porous lime-stone, vast chambers eroded and filled with water as sea levels rose and fell, creating the underground reservoirs. Over time, the vaults and their roofs col-

lapsed, thus shedding beams of sunlight on the crystalline waters. Visible from the ground through mysterious-looking holes in the earth, or partially obscured by a tangle of tree roots, *cenotes* are revealed in a variety of shapes and sizes. Surface water is sometimes only an arm's-reach from the ground opening, while other *cenotes* must be approached by long, tunnel-like apertures that require a steep descent along stone-carved steps to their watery depths.

For the collection of rainwater, the ancient Mayans designed large *chultunes*, or cisterns, that collected rain in and around central plazas. The aid of gravity in this endeavor was paramount—the plazas were built to slope towards cisterns for easy collection. Many of these are still present today, including the Maya *chultunes* at Uxmal, Yucatán.

In the Spanish Colonial era, a sophisticated system for water collection and irrigation was vital to the existence of the working hacienda, for inhabitants as well as for livestock, orchards and fields. Its infrastructure—large water tanks, cisterns, and aqueduct channels—as well as its decorative features—fountains, ponds and dramatic reflecting pools—became prestigious symbols of high production and prosperity.

Built adjacent to *cenotes*, or wells, haciendas tapped into these natural resources and also made use of them as property markers. Water was

**Water lilies are at home in the *bebedero* at Hacienda Chan Poxilá, designed by Alejandro Patrón.**

The enchanting pool at Hacienda San José Cholul is sealed with *chukum* and draped with a hammock.
Designed by Salvador Reyes Ríos.

originally brought to the surface by mule (harnessed to a wooden wheel-pulley system), then later via windmill or electric pump. Many aqueducts today are still powered by windmills, as evidenced at Hacienda Sodzil, where windmills bring water to shaded stone channels that feed ponds and garden features. In fact, windmills became a common landmark of the Yucatán Peninsula landscape between 1920 and 1970.

On working haciendas in the Yucatán, rainwater cascaded down sloping roofs that funneled water into *caños*, or rainspouts, that spilled into cisterns or holding tanks typically located below terraces or patios. The water was channeled into either interior or exposed pipes, depending on the era. During the colonial epoch, ceramic pipes that led to underground cisterns were inserted into walls, a method that required drawing water from buckets. At the turn of the twentieth century, exposed galvanized pipes served as roof spouts to channel water into aboveground, cylindrical stone or concrete structures. Faucets enabled convenient access to this water for human consumption.

A hacienda's aboveground *tanques*, or tanks—many of which have been converted to splashy pleasure pools today—fed gravity-based aqueduct systems that irrigated livestock

A stone *caño*, or spout, spills water into the stone-lined *bebedero* below.
OPPOSITE: Hacienda Petac's *bebedero* was restored by Salvador Reyes Ríos as a dramatic water feature.

*bebederos* (troughs) and long expanses of orchards. A property's main water tank had to be high enough for gravity to move water long distances through channels of varying heights. Beyond the watering of fields and animals, water was also vital for machine cooling throughout the henequén period (1880–1910), during which steam engines were utilized to operate the fiber-extracting (*desfibradora*) machines.

Tanks appeared in a variety of sizes and shapes. Most designs were square or rectangular, although round tanks were built at Hacienda Chunchucmil and Hacienda San Antonio Tehuitz. Some estates had multiple tanks, as on the vast grounds of Hacienda Petac, which also features a forty-foot-long *bebedero* in the main corral. The stone walls that once surrounded the water tank at Hacienda San José Cholul have been preserved in crumbling splendor to partially seclude the intimate swimming pool. The original, rectangular *tanque* at

Hacienda Xcanatún was adapted by architect Ginés Laocirica into a scintillating new water space that features Jacuzzi jets and an impressive water wall at the south end.

In Valladolid, Casa de los Venados has been brought back to life with architectural renovations that allow the flow of water inside and out. Owners John and Dorianne Venator worked with architect William Ramírez to create a fusion between the home's colonial heritage and contemporary design elements. The seventeenth-century home features a central patio with a newly designed *macedonia*-stone fountain. A second, adjacent patio is anchored by a swimming pool that also bridges the gap between old and new: a walkway stretches over the pool and water flows into streams that run through a vaulted-roof passage, bringing the motion of water to all corners of the outdoor space. Ramírez also designed guest bathrooms with

At Casa Santa Ana, a fountain designed by Salvador Reyes Ríos flows into a canal sealed with *chukum*.
OPPOSITE: Tropical plants and an old stone wall envelop an outdoor bath at Hacienda Itzincab.

stones in a garden grotto and cascaded from outdoor pools. It can even transport bathers—as evidenced by one home that features a pool passage to an interior bathtub.

Luxurious outdoor plunge pools have been soaking up popularity in new and restored Yucatán homes. First designed and integrated into some of the first haciendas-turned-resorts, the outdoor bath, or plunge pool, integrates the beauty of stone, nature and natural finishes.

The ancient Mayans utilized the region's native trees—including *chukum*, *pixoy* and open-air showers that feature fossil-stone floors and walls surrounded by tropical plants.

## BATHS

With its orientation to water and nature, it is no surprise that many Yucatán haciendas and homes feature outdoor showers, unique bathtubs and plunge pools. Thanks to innovative architects, new home designs have amplified the importance of water and brought its soothing sounds and movements closer to home. Today, water has been brought inside courtyards, run along walls, trickled around

RIGHT: Stone walls entwined in roots surround an outdoor shower at Hacienda Santa Rosa.

tzalam—to create both pigments and sealants that produced smooth waterproof mortars to line their *chultunes* (cisterns). Recent experiments and successful adaptations of these old-world construction and finishing techniques have been made by architect Salvador Reyes Ríos and Grupo Plan. Their pioneering efforts have brought back old recipes for use in modern architectural applications, including pools and Jacuzzis. *Pixoy,* one of the tree-resin-based sealants, is used with the addition of earthen pigments to seal and bond walls while adding a colorful layer that produces a natural patina. A number of colonial structures (Hacienda Ochil, Hacienda Uayamón and Hacienda Petac) have been restored using a combination paint of *pixoy* and *kancab,* a rich red earth found in southern Yucatán State. The resin from the *chukum* tree is used in a traditional recipe to create a smooth mortar impermeable to water. The use of "smooth *chukum*" creates tones of blue from light to dark, which intensify with water depth. Two varieties of *chukum*—white and red—can be mixed or used singly to evoke different coloring effects. Reyes and Grupo Plan utilized white *chukum* for the pool at Hacienda Temozón, their first collaborative restoration project, which resulted in a cream-white color tone. Additionally, a natural

Windmills bring water to shaded stone aqueducts that feed ponds and gardens at Hacienda Sodzil. OPPOSITE, TOP: Designed by Salvador Reyes Ríos, an intricate stone wall adds texture to a plunge pool.

"ink" pigment obtained from *tzalam* wood can be combined with white cement plaster to produce a color tone that harmonizes with surrounding elements. The pool at Hacienda Uayamón was treated with this tinted mortar to produce a light reddish-brown color that complements the *tzalam*-wood deck surrounding the pool.

Set amidst the dramatic backdrop of the estate's ancient stone walls, the plunge pools at Hacienda Itzincab and Hacienda Uayamón are also lined with red *chukum*. Situated only bare-foot-steps away from the interior guest rooms, the pools are draped in private, lush gardens of ginger and bamboo. The spout for the bath at Uayamón is fashioned from one of the estate's original *caños*, or stone channel pieces, that once carried water through the property's vast aqueduct system.

Designed and built by Francisco Faller, the colonial hacienda-style home shared by Faller and his wife Ann Walström de Faller is a tranquil haven that pays homage to the soothing sights and sounds of water, both inside and out. Anchored by a jade-green lily pond fed by stone aqueducts, the lush property is accented with water troughs and antique stone *pilas* that harbor exotic aquatic plants. One of Casa Faller's unique water features glows like a jewel in the

Architect Alvaro Ponce integrates indoor and outdoor spaces with garden-view showers.
OPPOSITE: A unique pool passage leads to an interior tub in the master bathroom at Casa Faller.

master bathroom: what appears to be a deep, light-filled bath is actually a secret entrance to the outdoor pool, allowing one to plunge underwater and surface either indoors or out. Surrounded by calming green walls and a view of an interior courtyard, this room is a true favorite.

At Hacienda Xcanatún, two guest suites feature organically shaped bathtubs hand-carved by local craftsmen and designed by owner Jorge Ruz. Softly lit by skylights, these luxurious spaces are surrounded by tall walls of Ticul stone tile and stone waterspouts that allow water to spill into the tubs from high above. The spacious bathroom floors also feature a stone tile pattern by architect Ginés Laocirica, inspired from original salvaged pieces found during the hacienda's restoration.

Motivated by the tropical climate of the Yucatán, designers of contemporary Mexican homes often integrate indoor and outdoor spaces through the creation of interior gardens. Architect Alvaro Ponce designs contemporary homes that feature open-air private gardens for bathroom spaces. Inspired by Polynesian gardens that adjoin bath spaces, the layout and design of Ponce's bathrooms allow direct access to secret courtyard havens, sometimes even through shower doors that open from transparent walls. More "enclosed" bathrooms are also designed to appear to be outdoors—squared in with a floor-to-ceiling transparent glass wall. Breaking from the design of wall-to-wall ceramic or marble tiling in bathrooms, Ponce prefers to use colored stucco on walls, accented with the textural warmth of stone tiles. Occasionally, sinks are hand-painted, as are stencils for wall decoration and definition.

In early written descriptions of Hacienda Santa Rosa, research historian Blanca Paredes discovered that the location of an original English-style bath space was in a corner of the hacienda's old corral, which now adjoins the nineteenth-century owner's house. Architect Salvador Reyes Ríos designed and placed an outdoor shower and plunge pool at this site, in keeping with its historical origins. During the work, Reyes found Santa Rosa's stone corral walls entwined with the roots of an ancient *alamo* tree, the presence of which became integral to his design of the naturalistic plunge pool and open-air shower.

Shafts of sunlight dramatically illuminate the water in Cenote Dzitnup. Photo courtesy Yucatán Government.
OPPOSITE: At Hacienda Xcanatún, water spills into a hand-carved stone tub designed by Jorge Ruz.

From above, under, within and without, water's reaches have been harnessed and channeled through the centuries, and the testament of stonework, basins, tanks, wells, pools and fountains are evidence of the constancy of its presence in the Yucatán region. In today's contemporary dwellings, gardens and restored haciendas, capturing water is no longer so laborious, but the physical history of its containment brings great pleasure and aesthetic awareness to current lifestyles and cultural identity.

TOP: The outdoor pool at Casa Faller features a swim-through passage to an interior bath.
BOTTOM: An old carved-stone spout leads from Hacienda Aké's original water tank.

An old water trough was converted to an attractive lily pond at Hacienda Poxilá.

The arcaded *portal* at Hacienda Xixim features a dining table and iron bamboo *jefe* chairs.
OPPOSITE: An iron bamboo segmented planter by Yucatán Bamboo.

GRACED WITH A WARM TROPICAL CLIMATE, THE OPEN-AIR SPACES OF THE YUCATAN—
ARCADED PORTALES, COURTYARDS, PATIOS AND DAYBED PAVILIONS—ARE AS
INTEGRAL TO A HOME AS ITS INTERIOR SPACES. THESE AIRY OUTDOOR ROOMS ARE
TRANQUIL SHELTERS FROM THE SUN AND LIBERATING SPACES IN WHICH TO ENJOY
THE SIGHTS, SOUNDS AND FRAGRANCES OF YUCATAN'S TROPICAL GARDENS.

# OPEN-AIR LIVING: PORTALES & GARDENS

**Portales, or covered porches** or walkways supported by columns or posts that lead to the entrance of a building, are a prominent architectural feature of Yucatán haciendas as well as colonial and contemporary homes. As with most architectural terms, the regional differences are many. The word *portal* most often refers to a large, covered space—sometimes also called a corridor or colonnade—with multiple columns or posts that provide main

access to a building. The term *pórtico* is also used, most commonly when the space is a single covered porch with one arch that leads to a main door or entry of a building.

Supported by stone columns or wooden posts, the *portal* extends the home's living space and is often the most used room in the house. *Portales* offer hammocks for resting, tables for dining and comfortable furnishings for idyllic respite. These broad, breezy areas are

The colorful *portal* at Hacienda Chan Poxilá features rocking chairs and Maya tortilla tables. Designed by Alejandro Patrón.

A rustic stone fountain punctuates a shaded pathway leading to the *portal* at Hacienda Santa Rosa.

enhanced by cool tile floors, ceiling fans and, often, views of water gardens. Many colonial *portales* feature hand-carved wooden hammock hooks embedded in walls, a testament to the historical and present-day practicalities of hammock use, here lauded by U.S. Diplomat Brantz Mayer upon his visit to the Yucatán in the nineteenth century:

> [I] recommend to all of those among us who are disposed to travel to hot countries that they get themselves a hammock made of henequén. With one, you are lord and master of the situation; and surely there is no more luxurious a way to sleep in warm countries. One hangs it from the roof beams; and it is suspended above the ground, away from the walls and free of insects; it conforms to the body, adapting itself to each one of the limbs; cause it to move and its swaying lulls you, and you are fanned and refreshed by its smooth movement in the air.

Smoothed and worn, these hooks are still used for hammocks and hanging decorative elements.

**At Casa Faller, a soothing jade green *portal* invites repose with a relaxing hammock.**

On colonial estates, *portales* were designed to create a cooling transitional space in the home. They often spanned both sides of the *casa principal*, allowing favorable conditions for outdoor living at varying times of the day. With refreshing breezes and changing light and shadow, these spaces become ever-changing rooms that are transformed from sunrise to sunset.

Views to luxuriant courtyard gardens, corrals, fountains or pools add to the sense of living outdoors. In addition to comfortable chairs and tables, many homes and haciendas furnish their outdoor spaces complete with lighting, paintings and treasured relics. Decoratively, these areas range from rustic and relaxed with well-worn leather *butacas* (traditional sling chairs) and three-legged Maya tortilla tables, to more sophisticated and elegant with ornate chandeliers, antique rocking chairs and tall iron plant stands. In addition to the prominent use of decorative stone elements, including crosses and saints, a variety of old stone vessels such as water filters and *pilas* (troughs originally used to water or feed animals) are put to use as planters.

Framed by distinctive arches, the *portal* of the Seijos' colonial home features an elegant grouping of white wicker chairs and tables that rest on a sea of French-patterned cement tiles. Surrounded by lush tropical gardens and myriad potted plants, the outdoor living space is the center court of the colonial home. Resting in one corner is an ornate white iron birdcage housing exotic birds that bring song to the shaded space. Topped with native plants, a large collection of old stone *metates* (grinding stones) line the *portal*, and yet another grouping of potted plants surrounds a hand-carved cross and decorative iron ornament.

A sea of French-patterned tiles and luxuriant plants enliven the arcaded *portal* at Casa Seijo.

Francisco Faller and Ann Walström de Faller's Mérida home is an inviting open-air hacienda built and designed by Faller in Yucatecan Colonial style. Their hacienda and others raised circa 1560 to 1800, before the upsurge of the sisal industry, are characterized by open areas in all

tral *sala* is enlivened with an intriguing collection of the couple's heirlooms, artifacts and antiques. Copper lanterns, horse tack, rope and deer antlers hearken to Francisco's love of sailboats and horses, his hunting prowess and talent as a ropemaker. Next to Yucatecan

the rooms. Three Moorish-style arches, which replicate those at Hacienda Noc Ac, mark the entrance to the heart of the home, a breezy open-air room that looks out onto orchid-filled gardens and a courtyard swimming pool. The cen-

painted crosses, leather *butacas* with timeworn patinas and Ann's heirloom trunks, the room expresses history both personal and architectural. Off the home's master bedroom, a *portal* painted in a soothing jade green invites repose

**Elegant Moorish arches draped with *fistus* vines frame the open-air *sala* at Casa Faller.**

unique stone vessels that allow exotic aquatic plants to be introduced into a home environment. Banana trees from Belize, Egyptian papyrus, mango ferns, heliconia and water hyacinths all flourish in Yucatán's climate. Innovations also abound in the use of Yucatán's indigenous *henequén agave*. Landscape designer Alejandro Chimal designed a mysterious "*henequén* maze" with the strategic placement of plantings at Hacienda Temozón.

ABOVE, LEFT: Hacienda La Pinka's colorful *portal*.

ABOVE, RIGHT: Old stone vessels punctuate the lush grounds at Hacienda San Antonio Cucul.

OPPOSITE: A carved wooden altarpiece frames a crucifix beneath the colorful *portal* at Hacienda La Pinka.

ABOVE: At Casa de Yturbe, a colorful painting by Sylvia García Aguilar brightens a tranquil *portal*.

OPPOSITE: A carved-stone serpent keeps a watchful eye on the gardens at Casa de Yturbe.

Alvaro Ponce is a leading Mérida architect noted for his contemporary homes that creatively integrate interior and exterior spaces. His designs feature multiple garden spaces throughout the home that adjoin bathrooms, anchor *portales* and enliven passages to bedrooms—a favorite location in which to position fragrant plants such as jasmine and mariposa.

Ponce's creativity extends to exterior landscapes as well. His designs feature chinked-stone garden walls, stone basins for aquatic plants and luxurious lawns with stone grids for sculptural interest.

Many outdoor patios and pergolas (free-standing covered spaces) are integrated with nature as vines and flowers spill from old stone *pilas* or climb up and onto ceilings. Casa San Juan in Mérida is resplendent with tropical plants climbing alongside an eclectic collection of old iron and stone elements. At Hacienda Xcanatún, Thai-style gardens designed by the owners in collaboration with Barbara and Giancarlo de Silvestri envelop the restored estate, radiating an exotic flavor with formal accents that include a *petanque,* or bocce ball court, in the *potrero* garden. A large iron birdcage was built on top of a portion of Xcanatún's old aqueduct and humorously designated as "Suite 319."

BELOW: Designed by Alvaro Ponce, this contemporary home features a *portal* with a unique courtyard.
OPPOSITE: An antique stone basin filled with water lettuce anchors this tranquil open-air space.

Yucatán's open-air spaces celebrate the region's relaxed lifestyle. Not just for socializing and dining, outdoor spaces provide for lounging or sleeping as well as cooking and bathing. Rooftop terraces and outdoor baths and pools are considered vital to the Yucatán outdoor-living landscape. The soothing sound of water is also a common feature. Further description of many of these features is included in the Water Spaces and Coastal Homes chapters.

Original French floor tiles, beamed ceilings and antiques grace Casa Seijo's elegant portal in Mérida.

OPPOSITE: A remate de escalera poses as garden sculpture at Casa Seijo.

A POWERFUL SENSE OF ROOTEDNESS PERVADES YUCATECAN HOMES AND GARDENS.

# CASAS YUCATAN

**The region's history and natural resources** are transfused easily from exterior landscape through to a home's interiors, resonating a feeling of permanence and a connection to age-old traditions in spite of contemporary adaptation. Many common denominators come into play: the prominent use of stone as building material and intricately carved details, architectural solutions to encourage ventilation with *portales* and courtyards, and

a bold use of color long favored by the Mayans. Lime stucco was also used for special decorative details.

The variety of homes in this chapter fall into the following three categories: Colonial, Porfiriato and Mexican Contemporary. The Colonial style of construction, which began with the Spanish Conquest and lasted well into the nineteenth century, was only overshadowed during the Porfiriato era (1880–1910), so named for Mexican President Porfirio

Díaz. A prosperous time in Mexico's history, this epoch embraced ornate European decorative influences in both architecture and furnishings. In addition to the ancient walled city of Campeche in Campeche State, the peninsula's oldest homes are found throughout Yucatán's many colonial cities, including Mérida, Valladolid, Tekax and Izamal. These five cities were represented as five stars on the nineteenth-century Yucatecan flag, as the Yucatán was then a republic independent of Mexico.

## Casa Seijo

The colonial home of Jorge and Maricela Seijo was built between 1750 and 1780. Its façade and interiors were later modified with more ornate French details during the Porfiriato era. The grand elegance of the fourteen-room home is in its tall ceilings, carved doors, French-tile floors and arcaded *portal* that wraps around two sides of the interior courtyard. Antique furnishings include French mirrors, chandeliers and family heirlooms. The principal dining room features Italian Renaissance furniture, paintings from Spain, antique French porcelain, and hand-cut crystal. A second dining room reveals a colorful collection of contemporary paintings juxtaposed

**Colonial treasures are at home at Alberto's Continental Patio in Mérida.**

amidst an antique *vargueño* (traveling writing desk) and leather chairs that glow with the warmth of time-hewn patinas.

Outside on the shaded *portal*, a casual comfort balances the sophisticated setting with a profusion of plants and an inviting cluster of rocking chairs. Jorge Seijo's enthusiasm for cultivating tropical plants is evident in his lush courtyard garden filled with antique stone water vessels, cisterns and old architectural elements newly posed as garden sculpture.

## Casa de los Venados

Casa de los Venados (House of the Deer), the colonial home of John and Dorianne Venator, is a majestic property located less than a block from Valladolid's central plaza. Rescued by its owners in early October 2000, the seventeenth-century home was originally built by the mayor of Valladolid and abandoned in 1964. Enamored with its splendid proportions and architectural details, the Venators vowed to rescue it for posterity and bring it back to life. With architect William Ramírez, they developed an ambitious restoration plan that blends old and new, bringing together modern comfort and contemporary details in a historic setting.

The recently restored colorful façade of Casa de los Venados features unique contemporary doors.

As avid collectors of both Mexican contemporary and folk art, the Venators will extend their home as a venue for many performing and visual art functions, as well as for occasional use by Yucatán art museums as a remote gallery. The property is also a promised gift as a restricted bequest to The Mexican Fine Arts Center Museum of Chicago. The eighty-foot-long *sala* boasts dramatic twenty-five-foot-high ceilings and a newly added musician's balcony—an ideal backdrop in which to host musical concerts. Myriad interior courtyards showcase newly designed water features, pools and stone fountains that create a soothing outdoor environment for the home's five two-story bedroom suites and single two-bedroom apartment. A rooftop deck will provide views of the old cathedral across the street.

## Quinta El Olvido

Quinta El Olvido was designed and built at the turn of the twentieth century by the same illustrious team of architects and engineers that constructed Mérida's renowned Governor's Mansion and Peón Contreras Theater. Its ornate French-Italian–influenced decoration is representative of the Porfiriato period and features an elaborate roof parapet and decorative balustrades.

Owner Jorge Trava's regal home is spacious and grand: five social areas, five bedrooms, five bathrooms, two dining rooms, and two kitchens. The interiors feature colonial floor tiles, ornately plastered columns and a Baccarat chandelier that holds court in the grand salon. Family portraits line the walls, and decorative objects from Czechoslovakia, Italy, France and Spain are at home throughout.

An antique Greek ceramic vase postures in an ornate *nicho* at Quinta El Olvido.
The grand *sala* at Quinta El Olvido is resplendent with regal treasures, including a Baccarat chandelier.

Old stone walls enclose the central courtyard, and a Maya embroidered pillow accents a woven fiber chair.

Millet's plan of action was to first restore the roof using the original colonial technique of *bah-pec* (building a lime and limestone roof) supported by *rollizos* (round beams). A central courtyard roof was preserved, keeping its original exposed stucco. Subsequently, all interior spaces were renovated within the home's original layout.

Also conceived by Josefina Larraín and Salvador Reyes Ríos, the interiors were designed to re-create the feeling of the colonial epoch, particularly in the color choices and textures. Walls were painted the traditional Yucatecan blue of the nineteenth century. Local tropical woods were used for furniture and accessories, and chandeliers and candelabras were custom crafted from hand-forged iron. As the central stone courtyard encompasses the house in a feeling of being outdoors, woven-fiber armchairs were chosen for both the outdoor dining space and interior living room.

**A lushly planted courtyard, designed by Josefina Larraín, looks onto the ancient ruins of the Izamatul pyramid.**

## Casa Reyes-Larraín

In many of Mérida's older downtown neighbor-hoods, nobly decorated Porfiriato-era homes are being rescued and restored through the efforts of an artistic community committed to the preservation and appreciation of the neighbor-hood's architectural heritage. The Reyes-Larraín house is a testament to the strong potential that hundred-year-old homes possess for modern

Dating between 1905 and 1910, the home's façade and entrance foyer maintain the neoclas-sical eclectic style typical of the Porfiriato period. Inside, characteristic and ornate deco-rative details were found juxtaposed with sim-pler, utilitarian architectural elements, including *cañon* (flat-plank) doors. This unique blend of luxury and practicality was preserved in the owners' renovation plan.

living, and an ideal example of the creative inno-vations incorporated in these houses. Owners and designers Salvador Reyes Ríos and Josefina Lar-raín rescued their Porfirian treasure from neglect and vowed to honor the spirit and origins of its architectural history in their restoration concept.

Reyes and Larraín focused their careful restoration on a balance between old spaces with new uses and new spaces with old uses, expressed through architectural choices. Every new compo-nent or element introduced was designed to pre-serve the original space's proportion, scale and

Old iron wheels from hacienda machinery rest as sculpture in the Reyes-Larraín courtyard.

OPPOSITE: A water garden surrounds an old well in the center of the colorful courtyard.

Designed by Salvador Reyes Ríos, the bathroom suite at Casa Reyes-Larraín
is anchored by washbasins set within a tropical hardwood table.

OPPOSITE: The elegant dining room is kept refreshingly cool
by high ceilings and plenty of cross-ventilation.

leveling and the introduction of pipes, they were carefully set aside. As all the tiles were not salvageable, the owners found an innovative solution for the new floors in all the rooms: a large array of the old intact tiles were re-laid in the center of the floor and a polished-cement frame was set to enclose the patterned tiles, giving the appearance of a "rug" of mosaic color. Some remaining original tiles were put to new use as decorative accents in shower-wall niches in the home's bathrooms.

The kitchen's striking color and tile graphics add to the lively hum of daily cooking activity and make it the jewel of the house. The twenty-foot ceiling and the counter with its arches and dramatic hood replicate colonial dimensions and style. On the counter, designer Larraín used a combination of traditional Talavera tiles from Puebla, creating an overall modern statement with the unique combination of patterns.

The main bathroom suite is composed of a common hall with courtyard access. To divide the room, a new wall plastered with a *chukum* finish was constructed, creating two separate shower/toilet units. In the hallway, ceramic wash basins are set inside an eight-foot-long table crafted from *machiche*, a tropical hardwood.

A carved-stone basin with beautiful texture, designed by Alvaro Ponce, accents a Yucatán garden.

OPPOSITE: This interior courtyard features an intricate, stone-chinked wall and fragrant tropical plants. Residence in San Antonio Cucul.

## Casa de Yturbe

Enclosed behind tall white walls, the Mexican contemporary home of Luis and Laura de Yturbe luxuriates in open spaces. Designed by architect Jesús García Collantes, the Mérida home rises up to high ceilings and expands in wide, open corridors that encourage ventilation. Water is a soothing and strategic presence in the house. A central courtyard that welcomes with its aqua-blue fountain is surrounded by a series of white arcades laden with bougainvillea. Tucked into a nearby corner is a reflecting pool, viewed from the dining room and bedrooms through floor-to-ceiling glass windows. A stone Virgin watches over this tranquil haven, her statuesque stillness heightening the effect of the constantly moving shadows crossing the space, thanks to the large wooden beams overhead. The swimming pool, on the opposite side of the house, provides the entire east side with a pleasing, cooling view, particularly from the shady eighty-foot-long *portal*.

Colorful paintings, potted plants and Mexican furniture line the generously proportioned corridors that lead to the home's living and dining areas, four bedrooms, office and back *portal*. An eclectic mix of contemporary art, stone sculptures and pre-Hispanic elements enliven the home's open-air spaces. Adding

Old Maya *metates* rest atop a *sabino* (Mexican cypress) bureau at Casa de Yturbe.

OPPOSITE: A *bóveda* ceiling and nineteenth-century painting add old-world interest to Casa de Yturbe.

architectural interest to the sixty-five-foot-long dining and living room is a masterful brick *bóveda* (vaulted) ceiling, crafted by artisans from the state of Jalisco. Its presence decorates the room with a rich feeling of Mexican craftsmanship.

## Homes by Architect Alvaro Ponce

In the Mexican contemporary homes designed by architect Alvaro Ponce, the welcome is warm, and homage to Yucatán's natural materials and their infinite textures is visible and palpable throughout. Ponce combines timeless materials in new and inventive ways, infusing them with modern-day comfort and distinctive details to make each home unique. Finding inspiration in both Mexican Colonial and Balinese homes that focus on bringing nature inside through courtyards and interior water gardens, Ponce's signature designs focus on a true integration of architecture, furnishings and gardens. He adeptly hand-designs custom architectural elements, including doors, iron gates, light fixtures and carved-wood columns inspired by those seen in Antigua Guatemala. Ponce's influence also extends to gardens, pools and decorative outdoor elements, such as copper planters, stone water basins that echo colonial *pozos* (wells), and baptismal fonts, specially aged with earthen pigments to meld into the landscape.

In Hacienda Sodzil, Alvaro Ponce designed a residence to embrace the owners' love of nature, open-air living and entertaining. The 10,000-square-foot home faces inward to surround a spectacular contemporary pool, garden and *palapa* (a thatched-roof open-air structure). Visible from every room in the house, the sparkling, cobalt-blue pool is both water haven and sculpture. The modern design is an impressive feat of engineering and spans thirty-six feet. Reflecting into the long span of water are the massive geometric shapes from a Ticul-stone wall that progressively decrease in size in precise, smooth sections.

The elegant arcaded *portal* holds court as the heart of the home, incorporating both dining and living areas. The owners' favorite outdoor "room," the *portal* is anchored on both ends by textural garden spaces that glow with sunlight from above. Floors of *fiorito* (crosscut travertine) and hand-chinked walls blend contemporary polish with the colonial traditions of *rajueleado* (stone-chinked surfaces). Playing a large role in the lives of the home's owners, contemporary Mexican paintings and artworks line the rooms and corridors of the home. In addition to classic landscapes and modern sculpture, their collection also features an early Carlos Mérida painting, one of his few

Designed by Alvaro Ponce, this elegant home in Hacienda Sodzil features a colorful entrance that leads to an inviting courtyard lined with *macedonia* stone columns and lush, tropical plants.

OPPOSITE: This lush inner courtyard leads to the dramatic front doors of this contemporary home in Hacienda Sodzil.

Architect Alvaro Ponce created a graceful, open-air *portal* to enjoy lush garden and pool views. Residence in Hacienda Sodzil, interior design by Vivian Hedges, New York.

figuratives painted early, before he became known for his geometric abstracts.

Surrounded by fragrant mariposa and secluded off the master bedroom, the private porch is a favorite place of respite for the owners. Its shaded relaxing view looks onto the gardens and pool. Only steps away from the pool, the master bathroom provides easy access to it through a private garden courtyard. The master bedroom's elegant *bóveda* ceiling and subdued lighting create a refreshingly cool atmosphere. The high walls are accented by a hand-painted floral pattern inspired by fabrics found by the

owners. The decorative addition of hand-painted details throughout the home was prompted by one owner's memories of her grandmother's colonial Mérida home that featured decorative stencils.

The contemporary home Ponce designed for its owners in San Antonio Cucul is a masterful balance of artistic treasures, architectural details and soothing garden spaces. Setting the stage for the home's prodigious use of stone textures, iron accents and rich color pigments is its front entrance. Massive wooden doors are surrounded by an intricate replica of a colonial stone *marco* (door surround). Its ornate carving is juxtaposed

A spectacular pool designed by Alvaro Ponce is both water haven and sculpture in Hacienda Sodzil. The Ticul-stone geometric shapes are a masterful progression of precise, smooth sections.

This peaceful master bedroom in Hacienda Sodzil
features a *bóveda* ceiling decorated with hand-painted floral designs.

Holding court beside a lush interior garden is an antique
ivory horse. Residence in San Antonio Cucul designed by Alvaro Ponce.

with ocher stucco walls and iron window grilles, reflecting the home's Mexican craftsmanship.

The house's gracious entrance gallery holds court with the soothing sound and sparkle of a bubbling floor fountain that rises up amidst a cluster of stone spheres in varying shades of cream-white and rich deep orange. Overhead,

recessed lighting plays up the patterns in the impressive *bóveda*, which adds dimension to the art-filled entrance. Throughout the home, a vast art collection reveals the owners' fondness for Mexican contemporary paintings, sculpture and unique antique objects, including an ivory horse from India. Hand-painted designs by Humberto Hou also serve to decoratively accentuate the walls and doorways. Ponce's attention to designing with light and shadow is also a pleasing element in the three interior courtyards that dance with striped light throughout the day.

Honoring the influences of Mexican architect Luis Barragán, Ponce designed three Mérida homes—Casa Madina, Casa Sansores and Casa Maiz—that celebrate the bold use of color and the play of light and shadow. Each property features a multilevel layout, providing an open feeling to the house while allowing each room its own mood and "sensation" with the spatial separation of a few steps. In addition to floor-to-ceiling glass windows that flood corridors and rooms with natural light and garden views, skylights also play an important role in Ponce's homes. At Casa Madina, Ponce designed a dining room interior with a stepped wall of potted plants bathed in overhead natural light and bright pink paint. His fondness for bright colors was also employed

at Casa Sansores, where rich colors are splashed on focus walls and wall *nichos*. The outdoor spaces at Casa Maiz create a pleasing oasis for the family home: an inviting pool rests next to an adjacent open-air *palapa*, which features a hand-painted floor and nearby changing room with a garden shower open to the sky.

The entrance at Casa Sansores features a lily pond and Ticul ceramic pots. Designed by Alvaro Ponce.
OPPOSITE: Bold color is at home inside Casa Sansores with this brightly painted skylit room.

The rail system once used to transport *henequén* runs beneath a Moorish arch at Hacienda Ochil.

OPPOSITE: Elegant merlons decorate a building at Hacienda Yaxcopoil.

THE YUCATAN PENINSULA IS AN EPICENTER OF HACIENDA ACTIVITY AS THE INTEREST IN PRESERVING THESE ARCHITECTURAL JEWELS CONTINUES TO RISE AND MAKE NEWS.

# HACIENDAS

**In the three years since the publication** of our book *The New Hacienda*—which heralded the beginnings of the restoration renaissance— renovations have contin- ued in record numbers as more pioneering individ- uals have discovered the seductive allure of the hacienda era: its his- tory, its colonial design elements, its grand-scale interior spaces. As they have received favorable international press, the first haciendas to be

restored as luxury hotels and restaurants have been a catalyst for showcasing the charms of the hacienda design style to travelers worldwide.

Due to its popular- ity, the hacienda style and its signature charac- teristics have been widely emulated throughout the U.S. and other parts of the world. Elegant high- ceilinged rooms accented with hand-hewn *rollizos* (round beams), elegantly spartan *salas* with cool cement tile floors, broad *portales* with rustic furnishings, and a profusion of time-smoothed wood, wrought iron, and stone can now be seen in homes worldwide.

Decoratively, hacienda interiors contain elements from widely different eras, juxtaposed to explore connections and celebrate contrasts. In *portales*, Maya stone *metates* and water troughs rest next to heavy, colonial leather trunks. French light fixtures dangle over Italian marble tables and locally made chairs. Artwork ranges from colorful contemporary paintings and religious *santos* to nineteenth-century pieces from Peru and Europe.

Industrial relics from the Yucatán's *henequén* era—wooden machine molds, iron wheels and water pumps—hold unique appeal as decorative artifacts. Small wheels are set into newly constructed walls as window guards, and old iron-rail tracks once used to transport *henequén* from field to processing house have been fashioned into an entrance gate at Hacienda Nohchakan. Other architectural elements are pressed back into service in new roles: hand-carved corbels can support planters or trunks instead of roof beams; old stone irrigation-channel pieces become water spouts

for interior baths; iron scales and window grilles decoratively guard walls.

Innovations also abound as creative solutions are devised to reveal traces of a hacienda's past. Small sections of original stenciled walls might be left exposed for a glimpse of decorative history. Restored stuccoed walls also leave a few old stones exposed. At Hacienda Xcanatún, a new guest room was configured in a space that once featured multiple doorways. To create sufficient wall space for placing a bed, owner Jorge Ruz chose to have one doorway filled, yet left recessed a few inches from the wall plane. This shallow *nicho*, centered behind the bed frame, is an echo of the room's original doorway.

## Hacienda Uayamon

A new arrival on the hacienda revival scene is Hacienda Uayamón, located in the state of Campeche. Translating to "place of the tender *huayas*" (a local fruit tree), Uayamón is a distinctive property that abounds with restoration innovations and new uses. Conceived by Grupo Plan as a luxury hotel, Hacienda Uayamón features ten *casitas* housed in former workers' houses, two luxury suites set inside the old

**Hacienda Uayamón's former infirmary was converted to luxury suites complete with private plunge pools.**
**OPPOSITE: Restored by Salvador Reyes Ríos, a dramatic stairway leads to the elevated *casa principal*.**

infirmary, and a restaurant and library in the *casa principal*. The choice to leave the old private chapel and *casa de máquina* (machine house) in partial ruin adds special character and a vivid sense of history to the estate. Their roofless structures and multiple arches are shrouded in vines and bathed in sunlight, standing as architectural sculptures.

The Uayamón pool was another creative design by architect Salvador Reyes Ríos and Grupo Plan devised to show off the hacienda's past: water now flows between the original stone walls and columns, built to support the roof of an ice factory that was never completed. The spacious

**Hacienda San Antonio's restored *casa de máquina* (machine house) exudes a commanding presence.**

Magnificent stencils decorate the bathroom walls of a former watchtower at Hacienda San Antonio.

A guest bedroom at Hacienda Xcanatún features a *nicho* that stands as an echo of the original doorway.

OPPOSITE: A richly colored wainscoting lends warmth to the library at Hacienda San José Cholul.

daybed pavilions adjoining guest suites were also a solution to allow guests to commune with the natural jungle in a luxe, simple setting, complete with ceiling fans and lights.

## Hacienda San Antonio

Following an ambitious restoration, Hacienda San Antonio has evolved into a majestic estate that welcomes visitors to its luxurious grounds encompassing tranquil gardens, courtyards, ponds and pools. Nine guest rooms—beautifully decorated with furnishings that re-create the style of the early twentieth century—are housed within the hacienda's *casa principal*, *casa del encargado* (housekeeper's quarters) and former school. Owners Cándida Fernández and Eduardo Calderón were attracted to the hacienda's unique neo-Gothic architectural style and many of its original, still-intact design details. Originating in the seventeenth century as a cattle ranch, San Antonio was converted to a *henequén* hacienda around 1870. The estate underwent further expansion and remodeling in 1906, at which time the chapel was constructed and the *casa de máquina* and *casa principal* were remodeled. One of the highlights of the renovation was the discovery of several original wall stencils that were painstakingly documented and restored.

## Hacienda Petac

While researching our second book, *The New Hacienda*, we were captivated by the richness of the Yucatán region's hacienda architecture and the history of its multilayered civilizations. Trailing through myriad Maya villages and down overgrown dirt paths, we encountered many hacienda revivals in full force, as well as dormant treasures untouched by modern hands. In collecting photos and firsthand accounts of hacienda revivals, the idea of rescuing a hacienda from ruin and bringing it back to life took firm root—we were on a quest for a colonial hacienda that showed potential for restoration.

In early 2000, Hacienda Petac finally found us. An eighteenth-century estate in close proximity to Mérida, Hacienda Petac was a colonial cattle hacienda before its conversion to a *henequén* plantation in the late 1800s. Unlike many of the peninsula's haciendas that were altered over time, Hacienda Petac's architectural integrity was surprisingly intact, without any twentieth-century alterations. The fact that Petac predates many Yucatán haciendas that were built during the *henequén* boom of the late nineteenth century endows the estate with a rich colonial history. The juxtaposition of the

colonial *casa principal* to its later-built, nineteenth-century *casa de máquina* created a unique testimonial to Yucatán's diverse hacienda epochs.

Although many haciendas had their acreage dramatically reduced during the land reforms that followed the Mexican Revolution, Petac managed to maintain ninety original acres, all enclosed by dry-stack stone walls. The property was comprised of numerous workers' buildings, a chapel, water storage tanks, and a stone aqueduct system once used for orchard and field

Painted Maya crosses rest atop a colonial trunk at Hacienda Petac.

OPPOSITE: Hacienda Petac's *portal* features *butacas* and Moorish-style arches that frame garden views.

Hacienda Petac's *sala* is enlivened with melon-hued walls, deep-blue wainscoting and mint-green Astratiles.

At Hacienda Petac, stone-chinked walls present a textural backdrop for iron grilles and lanterns.

irrigation. The presence of some existing infrastructure (water, electricity, good roads) was an added attraction.

Despite its critical need for a new roof and massive facelift, Petac's potential for revival was immediately apparent. We saw a jewel in the overgrown jungle—rich in original architectural

lime plaster and stucco was also intact. The combination of these unique elements on a single property prompted us to consider the hacienda's value as a future showcase for Mexican design and hacienda restoration.

In the spring of 2000, we teamed up with Dev and Chuck Stern to partner a future for

elements and design details that had been essentially unaltered through time: baroque stone entrance arches, stucco ornamentation, exquisite Moorish-style arcades, interior wall stencils and hand-turned spindles on windows and doors. A stone lime kiln once used for making

Petac. As a foursome, our shared passions for Mexican history elevated the project into a dream in the making. From the beginning, our vision was to preserve Petac's architectural legacy. We wanted to create a venue for educating homeowners and designers in the spirit and details of

**Moorish-style arches and a decorative parapet grace the elegant façade of Hacienda Petac.**

an authentic eighteenth-century hacienda, while also forging a comfortable retreat that would hail the original richness and splendor of the Yucatán lifestyle. To these ends, we have sought unique antiques and elements that would best echo the hacienda's origins and reflect its rural surroundings. We imagined a place where home-owners and designers could come to discover architectural restoration and building tech-niques, Mexican antiques and local design resources—all a step away from the estate's luxu-rious pools and gardens.

With these goals in mind, we devised an over-all vision for the property that would accommo-date our dual missions. The *casa principal* would be used as a library and as common space for entertaining and dining. The machine house would be renovated for guest suites, an owner's apart-ment and a 1,200-square-foot billiards room. Additional guest rooms and a Mexican Design Center would be housed in revitalized buildings adjacent to the *casa principal*. The nearby village was a significant asset in the plan, providing local labor and staffing for hacienda projects.

In June 2000, initial work began with exten-sive clean-up and careful evaluation of what ele-ments would be salvageable for reuse during the restoration. Original paint colors were excavated and old beams, wood, stone and iron were metic-ulously sorted and stored for later use. Doors and spindled window-guards were cleaned and restored with special finishes, and traditional cement tiles were selected for floors. Carr and Witynski established a comprehensive interior design plan for the *casa principal* that would be true to the hacienda's roots and evoke a luxuri-ous timeless air. Traditional design elements were sought that would establish an air of authentic-ity and reflect the country setting. In keeping with the belief that it is color and architectural detail that truly furnish a room, the interior design focused on accenting rooms with simple colonial antiques and *santos* to achieve an understated elegance.

Architect Salvador Reyes Ríos, in partnership with a group of architecture and restoration pro-fessionals, worked with Carr and the Sterns to orchestrate and fine-tune the hacienda's new presence. The foundation for all the architectural design and engineering work was the maintenance of balance between historical restoration and modern adaptation. In addition to restoring the roof and installing air conditioning, technical issues included updating electricity and plumbing. The restoration plan integrated many traditional methods and masonry techniques, including the

**A Spanish-style table designed by Joe P. Carr anchors Hacienda Petac's elegant dining room.**

use of *cal* (lime-based paint) and ancient Maya stucco finishes.

The roof restoration spanned three months and required removal of its original fifteen-inch packed lime-and-stone base. As the old roof surface was removed, it expanded, eventually yielding a three-foot-deep refuse field of *caliche* that became the base material for a porch extension on the back *portal*. Removal of the original stone exterior's weathered stucco and careful restoration of its chinked-wall surface (*rajueleado*) was a six-month project. Technical issues included updating the electricity three times to accommodate air conditioning and a system of wells dependent on electrical pumps. The plumbing required new wells and septic systems in addition to five miles of pipes and trenches to support new bathrooms and garden irrigation. Despite the enormity of the task, the long-term restoration project has proceeded, thanks to the fortitude of a partnership enchanted by the special old-world charms of Hacienda Petac.

Sharing the partners' interest in creative reuse and salvage, Reyes and his group devised innovative solutions that would employ existing elements. To support the shade-giving pergola creatively designed to extend over the pool surface, old round beams were installed as posts,

enabling sun cover for the hammocks that dangle just above the water. Another massive beam and corbels found in the *casa de máquina* were recycled for decorative use above the kitchen counter. The colonial-patterned tiles discovered in one room of the *casa principal* were an assembly

Talavera tiles and culinary antiques add to the flavor of Mexican cooking traditions at Hacienda Petac. Local *calabazas* (squash) and purple onions hint at the preparations to come.

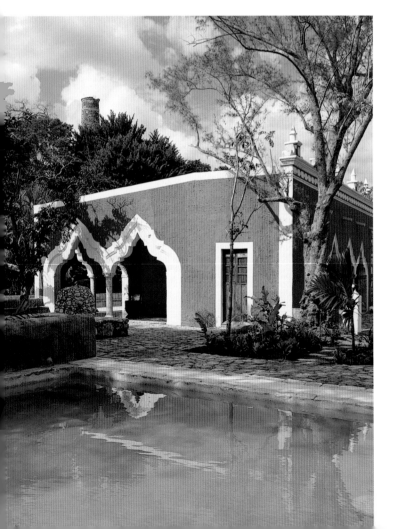

of useable and damaged cement tile. Wanting to preserve this colonial-patterned tile as a testament to the hacienda's decorative past, the Sterns had the pattern replicated and new molds fabricated. The original useable tiles were moved to the *casa principal*'s chapel and laid in a central field surrounded by a polished cement floor.

Addressing the placement of soothing water features was vital for surviving the Yucatán's tropical climate. First, the estate's former water storage tank was converted to a swimming pool and surrounded by a shade garden of native ferns and tropical plants. Original wells and aqueducts were retooled to feed the corral's forty-foot *bebedero* (water trough), which now splashes water from multiple stone *caños* (spouts) in a fountain display. For the *casa de máquina* building, Reyes designed a lily pond to surround the old chimney, as well as a thirty-six-foot-long water feature inspired by the water channels that once fed the orchards. Lined with Maya *chukum* stucco, a tree-resin blend noted for its permeability and natural translucence, the fountain's trickling water circulates from an elevated water chamber to a second source at ground level.

Once the estate's former irrigation tank, Petac's swimming pool beckons with a shady *pergola* and a view to the *casa principal*.

## Interiors

Although modest in size, the hacienda's *casa principal* is a grand space with high-beamed ceilings, thick walls, and doors opening onto two *portales* that overlook the main corral and gardens. A simple yet richly inviting room, the long, narrow central *sala* features melon-hued walls, deep-blue wainscoting and mint-green cement floor tile. The warmth is echoed in the antiques and furnishings crafted from tropical woods. Carr and Witynski collaborated with Salvador Reyes Ríos and Josefina Larraín on new custom-designed furnishings that would complement the antiques. Special attention was given to choosing fabrics and leathers that evoked a modest gentility, thus blending well with the older elements. The *sala*'s narrow-width, multiple doors and protruding hammock hooks presented a design challenge for positioning furniture. In addition to a nine-foot sofa, a narrow coffee table offered an appealing spatial solution, as did the custom mirror that accentuates the room's elongated shape.

The design of Petac's kitchen projects an admiration for traditional Mexican cooks and cuisine by featuring a collection of Mexican culinary antiques and offering an inviting space for regional cooking demonstrations. Bright yellow walls surround a rebuilt counter covered with colonial-style Talavara tile. A recycled beam and corbels, original to the hacienda, rest above the colorfully tiled counter. Dressing up the space with a utilitarian touch are old Mayan *metates*, sugar molds, a hand-carved coffee mortar, gourd-bowls, and a *repisa* for displaying glasses. A

pistachio-painted *copeti* discovered in Mérida has become a welcome, "working" art object, reemployed with the addition of hooks for utensil storage. The kitchen's original eighteenth-century treasure is an *alacena*, or built-in wall cabinet.

The original paymaster's office featured a unique wooden grille that was adapted to become

The estate's wooden "paymaster grille" was adapted to a new cocktail bar, designed by Salvador Reyes Ríos. Today, guests receive tropical drinks through the former payment window.

a decorative feature in the *casa principal*'s bar. Once a secure booth complete with a small window for money transactions, hacienda workers would receive their wages from their paymaster. In its original position, it divided a room in half and blocked traffic flow. The old booth was restored and newly positioned to form a central focal point for the custom-designed cocktail table.

One of the highlights of Petac's restoration was the discovery of a small chapel in the *casa principal*. The former owner intended the space for use as a bathroom. Only after our restoration began on the walls did the space reveal a plastered-over *nicho* in the center of the room. As its position was a profound clue to the room's original sacred use, the partners chose to restore the space as a chapel. Soon after, serendipity was with Carr in his discovery of a rare *santo*—perfectly sized to fit the tall *nicho* space. The blue hue of the hand-painted Virgin's robe was the same hue as the room's original paint, detected in the window jambs. Perhaps it was a coincidence, or perhaps, as we like to think, the color scheme of the original architecture and relics of this space was already perfectly worked out, just waiting to be brought to light.

**A low stone altar, *nicho* and antique *santo* contribute to the heavenly air of Petac's tranquil chapel.**

Designed by Alvaro Ponce, Casa la Madriguera's colorful entrance features carved columns and stone walls.

FROM THE PRISTINE BEACHES OF YUCATAN'S COASTAL VILLAGES TO THE CORAL REEFS AND SEASIDE TEMPLE RUINS OF THE MAYAN RIVIERA IN QUINTANA ROO, THE WARM, TURQUOISE WATERS OF THE PENINSULA ARE THEIR VERY OWN ATTRACTION.

# COASTAL HOMES

**Sailing, snorkeling and scuba add adventure** to the idyllic coastal pace while the flamingo-rich shores of Rio de los Lagartos and Celestún offer nature enthusiasts eco-friendly estuaries. Tucked amidst fishing villages, mangrove swamps and salt marshes on Yucatán's northern coast, beautifully designed coastal homes have drifted into the peaceful towns of Progreso, Chicxulub, Telchac Puerto and Dzilam de Bravo. A region rich in

natural resources, this sandy stretch also possesses a wealth of ancient history: the Mayans settled along this coast to harvest and collect valuable salt, which was traded throughout the Yucatán Peninsula and well into Guatemala. The nearby coastal ruins of Xcambó are a present-day reminder of this ancient Maya trading center.

Facing quiet, solitary beaches, these sun-drenched contemporary seaside residences and

open-air *palapas* exhibit various design influences, including styles from the Caribbean, Greek isles and Mexican Pacific. Use of masonry, wood and copper fixtures is a common theme. In tune with the rhythm of the warm waves, these homes take their cue from their idyllic surroundings. Nature's gifts of water, air and light meld indoor and outdoor life in a simple and comfortable design. Nature's elements are complemented by unique local textures: fine grass and palm-thatched roofs top outdoor dining pavilions, natural-fiber furnishings, tropical woods, *conchuela* stone, and pebbles and seashells for intricate floor mosaics.

For many homeowners and architects, keeping a beach home is like keeping a boat, as the high salinity of the area dictates careful selection of materials and design. Non-rusting building materials are used to discourage salt-air erosion. Large windows, open stairwells and skylights bring sparkling light inside every room, and open floor plans allow cross-ventilation. Perfectly practical tile floors, along with built-in sofas and benches, create the ultimate no-fuss beach retreat. Hammocks strung across breezy porches become instant *siesta* spaces.

Standing at the edge of the sea on a quiet beach in Chicxulub, Luis and Laura de Yturbe's family home embodies comfortable coastal elegance inside and out. Designed by architect Jesús García Collantes, the two-story beach home features bright white interiors and an open layout with wide corridors and breezy stairwells. Thick bands of pebbles define spaces and ripple across cool tiled floors. Bright, contemporary paintings add color to dining room and living room walls and throughout the spacious house.

For this active family of outdoor enthusiasts, the home reflects their love of water and nature. An oceanfront swimming pool is nestled amidst palms, a sailboat is always ready to go, and bamboo stables house horses for summer-morning beach rides. A spectacular rooftop not only offers infinite ocean vistas and a star-filled sky for evening entertaining, but it is also a passage for rainwater that

**A contemporary painting, seashells and pebbles add color and texture to the Casa de Yturbe dining room.**

A spectacular rooftop beckons with cushioned *bancos* and infinite ocean vistas at Casa de Yturbe.

Nestled amidst palms, the alluring pool at Casa de Yturbe offers sparkling ocean views.

variety of local delicacies, including *tikin'xic* (fresh fish barbequed in *achiote* sauce), tropical fruit gelatos and *cocada* (coconut dessert).

Another coastal home that is a beautiful integration of surroundings and interior space is Casa Sak-Ik, designed by architect Alvaro Ponce. Taking its design cues from the Greek isles, this Mediterranean-style home features multiple balconies that welcome sea breezes into every corner. Ponce creatively integrated water and vegetation into daily living spaces to satisfy the owner's desire to coexist with nature.

collects in cisterns, part of a water system modeled after those used in many Greek-isle homes. With its deep-blue cushioned *bancos* that appear to stretch out to sea, the rooftop is a favorite for sunset gatherings and dinners.

Adjacent to the house is Casita Feliz, an open-air pavilion that looks out to the pool and sparkling sea beyond. A large hand-painted mural by Yucatán designer Carlos Millet anchors one wall and re-creates a tranquil beachfront scene. Comfortable chairs and a built-in sofa surround a large hardwood table used for casual dinners featuring a

**Above, left: Designed by architect Alvaro Ponce, Casa Sak-Ik was inspired by Greek-isle homes.**
**Above, right: A natural seaside landscape leads to Casa Barlovento, designed by Alvaro Ponce.**

In order to protect the beachfront's silvester fauna, the home was built with a raised construction and long pier to reach the beach. The swimming pool and its soothing waterfall, surrounded by shady pergolas and grass-thatched *palapas*, make it possible to enjoy the outdoors at any time. Inside, *conchuela* stone and rich tropical hardwood accents were used to harmonize the cool and warm surfaces.

The design of Casa La Madriguera reveals strong Maya influences, and features creative use of grass-thatched roofs and porches. Also designed by Alvaro Ponce, this beachfront home is anchored by a striking yet graceful floor, designed by combining dark and light *fiorito* (crosscut travertine) with seashells. Outside, Ponce created a spectacular optical fusion of pool and ocean, thus producing an endless visual extension of the property.

Designed by Alvaro Ponce, a grass-thatched *palapa* offers soothing sea views at Casa Barlovento.
OPPOSITE: A sisal hammock swings in the ocean breeze at Casa La Madriguera, designed by Alvaro Ponce.

for owner Eneko Belausteguigoitia along the beach in Chicxulub. Hand-crafted furnishings maintain the focus on natural elements and a grand-scale *palapa* bridges the sparkling sea on one side and tennis court on the other—making it a natural spot for day-into-evening gatherings.

A Maya *casita*, designed by Salvador Reyes Ríos, features a hanging bed at Hacienda San José Cholul.

OPPOSITE: Tiers of thatched grass create an intricate pattern in the *casita*'s interior.

STRONGLY ROOTED IN ANCIENT TRADITIONS, PRESENT-DAY MAYA COMMUNITIES ARE TIED TO CENTURIES-OLD BELIEFS AND CUSTOMS PASSED DOWN FROM GENERATIONS.

# THE NEW MAYA HOUSE

**The beautiful simplicity** of the traditional Maya house—a single-room dwelling with rounded corners and a thatched roof—is a common sight throughout the thousands of rural hamlets that stretch from the Yucatán Peninsula and further south through Belize and Guatemala. As a true testament to their longevity, identical Maya house façades can be seen today in the ancient, relief stone carvings at Uxmal and Labná.

This powerful Maya vernacular has been reincarnated in Yucatán dwellings and landscapes as an intelligent fusion of past and present design. Distilled in the work of architect Salvador Reyes Ríos and Grupo Plan, today's new Maya house emerges as an enchanting blend of modern-day comfort and traditional forms. In this luxe variety, Reyes highlights the essence of the *casa Maya* with a virtuoso use of natural materials, patterns and colors—all echoing that which has come before.

The traditional Yucatán Maya house (nah) is typically apsidal in shape, although rectangular, oval or square plans are also seen. Construction styles vary depending on the specific living, cooking or work/storage uses of the particular structure. The most common framework consists

of vertical poles set within a limestone foundation. These upright poles are stuccoed for living areas, or left open for better ventilation, as in separate cooking structures. In regions where stone walls are more common, stone houses are either dry-stacked or stuccoed. Where larger trees are more plentiful, wooden planks sometimes replace small-pole construction.

The home can consist of one or two structures. A more prosperous home features two separate spaces in close proximity: the larger consists of a main living/sleeping room with minimum interior elements—hanging hammocks, wooden stools, trunks and an altar table. The second is a separate, covered cooking and eating area, which is located behind the main living space or sometimes under the extension of the main roof. If there's only one main building, living and cooking functions are combined under one roof.

Robert Wauchope, who recorded his travels to the Yucatán Peninsula in the 1930s, documented a number of traditional Maya homes in his book *Modern Maya Houses*. Here he describes the design of the interior he visited:

> *Most of the central part of a Yucatecan house is occupied by hammocks, which are slung between crossbeams or other conveniently located sturdier members of the house framing. When one enters a house he is invited to sit down in a hammock or on a short three-legged stool or on a little wooden seat with a concave surface, with which the house is plentifully supplied.*

Wauchope reiterates the significance of the house's hearth, where "most home activities

**Designed by Salvador Reyes Ríos, this Maya *casita* is a haven of simple luxuries and textures.**

**OPPOSITE: A dry-stacked stone wall surrounds this traditional Maya house.**

center." The hearth is "always situated in one end or corner of the house (or of the kitchen, if this is a separate structure)" and "is usually located near a mainpost. Sometimes there are two fireplaces in the same house, generally in the same end. One is used for cooking tortillas and the regular meals; water is kept hot or a stew kept simmering all day on the other, which is usually the smaller of the two. A small stack of wood is near the fireplace at all times and the fire rarely goes out during the day or night."

The lush grounds of Hacienda San José Cholul, Yucatán, provide the setting for four intimate Maya guest houses. While respecting the traditional elements of the Maya house, these new *casas Maya* radiate a modern serenity. The use of the ancient pairing of lime-based paint and earth, mixed to produce vibrant wall pigments, is another welcoming reflection of continuity with the ways of ancient Maya culture. Primed first with *cal*, a lime paint, walls were then layered with *kancab* (red earth), dug from the south-central region of

Yucatán State, to create a muted, natural texture. Traditional *techos* (roofs) of *zacate* (natural grass) and *guano* (palm fronds) shelter the Maya house and covered work areas.

The new Maya house follows tradition with a floor plan comprised of two apsidal-shaped rooms. The modern addition of an enclosed, light-filled hallway connects the first, larger bedroom/living space with the second, a bathroom suite. The hallway features a pair of hand-carved *macedonia* stone sinks that rest elegantly upon solid, square bars of *tzalam*, a local hardwood. The sinks were designed to echo the shapes of traditional Maya *pilas*, once used for animal feed and water. Tall louvered windows bring natural light into the hall and traditional wooden doors open to the tranquil garden pergola and private plunge pool.

In the presence of hand-carved stone, tropical hardwoods and natural fabrics, the guest house interiors, designed by Salvador Reyes Ríos, possess a timeless aura. Reyes's furnishing choices were inspired by the use of these richly textured

**Lime-based paint and earthen pigments contributed to this richly colored wall.**
**OPPOSITE: Designed by Salvador Reyes Ríos, a carved-stone sink rests atop a wooden base in this *casita*.**

elements as well as the simple, rustic shapes of tables and chairs typical in traditional Maya dwellings. In respect of this design, the television's presence in the guest rooms is cleverly disguised in a simple wood housing—recessed when not in use to resemble a side table. Bedside tables are aglow in light from carved onyx cylinders.

To create the dramatic, fifteen-foot ceilings, tiers of grass-thatch are hand-tied with *bejuco*, a strong local vine, resulting in an intricate overhead tapestry. A hanging bed, suspended by ropes and shaded in soft white netting, invites cradled repose. Cool floors of polished white cement are striped with strips of *pucté*, a brown-yellow tropical hardwood. Shuttered windows and ceiling fans encourage soft breezes and continuous ventilation in the heat of the day.

Designed as a quiet space, the bamboo pergola is strung with hammocks and affords a relaxing view of luxuriant flowering trees. Nearby, outdoor dining is encouraged with chairs and a small table. Only steps away is another soothing jewel: a Jacuzzi enclosed by a bamboo fence, with a profusion of heliconia plants and palms. This private plunge pool is lined with a soft *chukum* finish—an ancient Maya technique originally employed to line rainwater cisterns. Made from an old-world recipe including resin obtained from the

Colorful walls, bamboo, stone and a thatched roof create a strong design statement.
OPPOSITE: An inviting bamboo *ramada* shades this outdoor area at Hacienda San José Cholul's Maya *casita*.

*chukum* tree bark, lime and water, the water-resistant finish reflects light and magnifies the depth of the water.

Again inspired by the classic use of natural materials, Reyes designed a Maya garden shed for the Torre-Diaz home north of Mérida. Constructed of vertical wood poles placed in a stone foundation, the design was created to blend impressive 2.7-meter-high stone wall mixes the earthy tones of Yucatán's indigenous stone—both red and orange Ticul stone, *conchuela* and *macedonia*—creating a dramatic backdrop to the shed.

With thousands of Maya villages dotting the peninsula's landscape, the familiar image of thatched-roof dwellings is firmly rooted in the region. In addition to their new luxe and garden

harmoniously into the landscape and become integral to, rather than on the perimeter of, the garden environment. The thatched-roof shed features two open doorways for airflow. A cement floor is a simple solution for storage of materials, tools and supplies. Running four hundred meters around the Torre-Diaz property, an forms, the Maya house has also been adapted for use as a spa, as evidenced by Hacienda La Pinka's new Mayan Retreat & Day Spa. The Maya house's pure, architectural footprint continues to evolve into a new century, providing inspiration for a new generation of homeowners and design professionals, including architects and builders.

A new Maya-style garden shed finds inspiration in traditional forms at Casa Torre-Diaz.
OPPOSITE: Inside this *casita*, a bed hangs from ropes and breezes flow freely. Hacienda Santa Rosa.

# RESOURCES

On the following pages, we have compiled select listings of Yucatán hotels, haciendas, spas and restaurants. We are also proud to share with you special Yucatán contacts, including architects, designers, artists and product sources. We can provide additional referrals to Yucatán design sources and real estate contacts through our Web site.

We invite you to visit our gallery, **Joe P. Carr Design**, which offers Mexican colonial antiques and old architectural elements, including a variety of Yucatán doors, wrought-iron window grilles and gates, ceiling beams, and hundred-year-old wood flooring. In addition to antique trunks and tables, we also make custom hacienda tables in grand-scale proportions from reclaimed Mexican hardwoods. Decorative accents include Mayan crosses, *santos*, antique ceramics, and hacienda iron lighting.

Please visit our Web site www.mexicanstyle.com for Mexican travel highlights and design news, including hacienda restoration projects as well as new hacienda-style homes being built in the United States.

## www.mexicanstyle.com

**AUTHORS' ADDRESS**

JOE P. CARR & KAREN WITYNSKI
3267 Bee Caves Road
#107-181
Austin, TX 78746
(512) 370-9663 tel
(512) 328-2966 fax
www.mexicanstyle.com

**AUTHORS' GALLERY**

JOE P. CARR DESIGN
3601 Bee Caves Road
At Barton Springs Nursery
Austin, TX 78746
(512) 327-8284

KAREN WITYNSKI
ARCHITECTURAL & INTERIOR
PHOTOGRAPHY
(512) 370-9663

TOP: Authors Joe P. Carr and Karen Witynski. MIDDLE: A traditional Yucatán door.

BOTTOM: Antique ceramics, tables, trunks and architectural elements are showcased at Joe P. Carr Design.

# TRAVEL GUIDE

We have compiled this listing of special Yucatán hotels, hacienda resorts and restaurants from our years of traveling in the region.

While researching our second book, *The New Hacienda*, we were captivated by the Yucatán's hacienda architecture and the emerging preservation and restoration movement. In 1999, we began our own journey to find and restore an old hacienda in the region. In early 2000, an eighteenth-century estate named Hacienda Petac found us. A colonial estate before its conversion to a henequen plantation in the late 1800s, Petac showed great potential for renovation.

A natural step in our Mexican design research, our hands-on adventure with Petac's restoration and design was a rewarding three-year experience. Many of the old Mexican antiques and unique elements used in the hacienda design were found during our travels throughout the Yucatán and central Mexico. The project is detailed in our Hacienda chapter, beginning on page 140.

**AEROMEXICO RESERVATIONS**
(800) 237-6639 in U.S.
01 (800) 021-4000 in Mexico

**AeroMEXICO**®

## YUCATAN HOTELS

**LA MISION DE FRAY DIEGO**
Calle 61, #524
Col. Centro
Mérida, Yucatán
(999) 924-11-11
www.lamisiondefraydiego.com

**HOTEL CARIBE**
Calle 59, #500
Col. Centro
Mérida, Yucatán
(999) 924-90-22
www.hotelcaribe.com.mx

**CASA SAN JUAN BED & BREAKFAST**
Calle 62, #545-A
Mérida, Yucatán
(999) 923-68-23
www.casasanjuan.com

**HOTEL MEDIO MUNDO**
Calle 55, #533
Col. Centro
Mérida, Yucatán
(999) 924-54-72
www.hotelmediomundo.com

**HOTEL CASA DEL BALAM**
Calle 60, # 488
Mérida, Yucatán
(999) 924-21-50
(800) 624-8451 in U.S.
www.yucatanadventure.com.mx

**FIESTA AMERICANA**
Paseo de Montejo, #451
Mérida, Yucatán
(800) 343-7821
(999) 924-11-11
www.fiestaamericana.com

**CASA MEXILIO**
Calle 68, #495
Mérida, Yucatán
(800) 538-6802 in U.S.
(999) 928-25-05
www.mexicoholiday.com

**EL MESON DE MARQUES**
Calle 39, #203
Valladolid, Yucatán
(999) 856-30-42

Authors Karen Witynski & Joe P. Carr

## HOTELS IN QUINTANA ROO

**MAYA TULUM RETREAT & RESORT**
Km 5 Carr. Tulum—Boca Paila
(888) 515-4580 in U.S.
(984) 877-8638
www.mayatulum.com

**THE EXPLOREAN—KOHUNLICH**
Carretera Chetumal—Escarcega
(877) 397-5672 in U.S.
(525) 201-8333 in Mexico City
www.theexplorean.com

## RESTAURANTS
In Mérida:

**ALBERTO'S CONTINENTAL PATIO**
Calle 64, #482
Mérida, Yucatán
(999) 928-53-67

**PORTICO DEL PEREGRINO**
Calle 57, #507
Mérida, Yucatán
(999) 928-61-63

**CENACOLO**
Paseo de Montejo #473
Mérida, Yucatán
(999) 920-32-05

**LOS ALMENDROS** (5 locations)
Calle 50 #493
Mérida, Yucatán
(999) 928-54-59

**PANCHO'S**
Calle 59, #509
Mérida, Yucatán
(999) 923-09-42

**PANE E VINO**
Calle 62, #496
Mérida, Yucatán
(999) 928-62-28

**AMARO**
Calle 59, #507
Mérida, Yucatán
(999) 928-24-51

**ABOVE AND OPPOSITE:** La Misión de Fray Diego Hotel welcomes guests with its colonial charm and tranquil atmosphere.

**LODGE AT UXMAL**
Uxmal, Yucatán
(800) 235-4079 in U.S.
(999) 923-22-02
www.mayaland.com

## HACIENDA HOTELS

The Haciendas
The Luxury Collection
Starwood Hotels &
Resorts Worldwide Inc.
Owners: Grupo Plan

HACIENDA TEMOZON, Yucatán
HACIENDA SANTA ROSA, Yucatán
HACIENDA SAN JOSE CHOLUL, Yucatán
HACIENDA UAYAMON, Campeche

(999) 923-80-89 tel
(999) 923-79-63 fax
(800) 325-3589 toll free in U.S.
(800) 909-4800 toll free in Mexico
(52) 1-555-242-5650 outside Mexico
www.luxurycollection.com

**HACIENDA SAN ANTONIO**
Municipio Tixkokob, Yucatán
(999) 910-61-44
www.haciendasanantonio.com.mx

**HACIENDA TEYA**
Hotel—Restaurant—Events
Km 12.5 Carr. Mérida—Chichén Itzá,
Kanasín, Yucatán
(999) 988-08-01
www.merida.com.mx/haciendateya/

**HACIENDA XCANATUN**
Km. 12 Carr. Mérida—Progreso,
Mérida, Yucatán
(888) 883-3633 toll free in U.S.
(999) 941-02-13
www.xcanatun.com

**HACIENDA CHICHEN**
At Chichén Itzá Archeological Site
Chichén Itzá, Yucatán
(800) 624-8451 in U.S.
(985) 851-00-45
Balamhtl@finred.com.mx
www.yucatantravel.com

**Outside Mérida:**

HACIENDA XCANATUN
Casa de Piedra
Km 12 Carr. Mérida—Progreso
Mérida, Yucatán
(999) 941-02-13

HACIENDA TEYA
Km 12.5 Carr. Mérida-Cancun
Kanasín, Yucatán
(999) 988-08-01

HACIENDA OCHIL
Km 175 Carr. Mérida-Uxmal
Abala, Yucatán
(999) 993-99-77

KINICH KAKMO RESTAURANT
Izamal, Yucatán
(999) 954-04-89

**In Quintana Roo:**

YAXCHE
Calle 8 Norte
Playa del Carmen, Q. Roo
(984) 873-25-02
www.mayacuisine.com

## CULTURAL CONTACTS
## AND MUSEUMS

SECRETARIA DE TURISMO
Calle 59, #514
Mérida, Yucatán
(999) 924-93-89
www.mayayucatan.com

HACIENDA YAXCOPOIL
Museum & Parador
Km 186, Fed. Hwy 261,
Mérida-Uxmal, Yucatán
(999) 927-26-06
www.yaxcopoil.com

HACIENDA OCHIL
Henequén Museum & Restaurant
Km. 175 Carr. Mérida—Uxmal
Abala, Yucatán
(999) 993-99-77
(999) 923-80-89

**In Mérida:**
Museo de Antropología e Historia
Museo de Arte Moderno (MACAY)
Museo de la Canción Yucateca
Museo de la Ciudad
Museo de Arte Popular
Museo de Historia Natural
Museo de Dzibilchaltún

**Other Destinations and
Web Sites of Interest**

HACIENDA AKE
www.ruinasake.com

EXPRESO MAYA, Luxury Train
Service in Yucatán:
www.expresomaya.com

www.mayayucatan.com
www.hotelesyucatan.com
www.mayan-world.com
www.travelyucatan.com
www.campeche.com
www.mayanroutes.com
www.thenettraveler.com
www.travelyucatan.com/campeche.htm
www.travelyucatan.com/maya-riviera.htm

**Haciendas Available for Tours
and/or Special Events**
See www.mexicanstyle.com for
more information:
HACIENDA YAXCOPOIL
HACIENDA KANCABCHEN
HACIENDA SAN ANTONIO CUCUL
HACIENDA TAHDZIBICHEN
HACIENDA POXILA
HACIENDA TEPICH

## ARCHITECTS

REYES RIOS + LARRAIN + KONZEVIK
Restoration, Architecture, Design
& Landscape
Salvador Reyes Ríos
Josefina Larraín Lagos
Gabriel Konzevik Cabib
Calle 62, #419
Mérida, Yucatán
(999) 923-58-08
reyesrios@prodigy.net.mx

SALVADOR REYES RIOS
JOSEFINA LARRAIN LAGOS
Furniture Design, Tile Design,
Color Consulting
Calle 62, #419
Mérida, Yucatán
(999) 923-58-08
jlarrain@sureste.com

PLAN ARQUITECTOS
Luis Bosoms C.—Architect/Dir. General
Loma Bonita 7
Mexico D. F., Mexico 11950
(555) 257-0097
Luis.bosoms@grupoplan.com
www.grupoplan.com

ALVARO PONCE, Architect
Mérida, Yucatán
(999) 943-30-75
corvina@tponce.com

ALEJANDRO VALES GARCIA
Architect
Col. Itzimna
Mérida, Yucatán
(999) 926-80-38
avales@yuc.quik.com

WILLIAM RAMIREZ PIZARRO
Architect
Col. García Ginerés
Mérida, Yucatán
(999) 920-20-97

JESUS GARCIA COLLANTES
Architect
Col. Roma
Mexico D.F., Mexico
(555) 211-00-06

JOSE DE YTURBE, Architect
Col. Lomas de Barranca
Mexico D.F., Mexico
(555) 540-43-68
deyturbe@infosel.net.mx

Hand-painted ceramic tile by Azulejos Artesanales. Represented by Nina Long.

**JAVIER MUNOZ, Architect**
Calle 23, #192
Col. García Gíneres
Mérida, Yucatán
(999) 920-07-16
bonch@mid.cablered.com.mx

**ALEJANDRO PATRON, Builder/Designer**
Calle 35, #354
Emiliano Zapata Norte
Mérida, Yucatán
(999) 944-93-79

**GINES LAOCIRICA, Architect**
Mérida, Yucatán
(999) 922-58-04
lgyuc@yahoo.com.mx

**ROBERTO CARDENAS/ EDUARDO CARDENAS**
Cardenas Arquitectos
Calle 17 N., #199-D
Col. García Ginéres
Mérida, Yucatán
(999) 920-35-78
r1@cardenas2.as

## ARTISTS, DESIGNERS AND RESOURCES

**MARTY BAIRD, Artist**
2232 The Circle Street
Raleigh, NC 27608
(919) 833-2232
mmbaird@intrex.net

**SALVADOR REYES RIOS & JOSEFINA LARRAIN**
Design & Landscape Studio
Calle 62, #419
Col. Centro
Mérida, Yucatán
(999) 923-58-08
reyesrios@prodigy.net.mx

**JOAN DURAN, Artist**
Calle 51, #473
Mérida, Yucatán
(999) 924-18-01
vision51@cablered.net.mx

**CARLOS MILLET CAMARA, Designer/Artist**
Calle 30, #362
Col. Emiliano Zapata Norte
Mérida, Yucatán
(999) 944-10-82
milletdiaz@aol.com

**Nina Long/Tile Representative: ASTRATILE & AZULEJOS ARTESANALES WHOLESALE TILE & ACCESSORIES, INC.**
1902 Flagler Street
Tampa, FL 33605
(813) 248-0455
ninalong@gte.net
www.wholesaletile.biz

**YUCATAN BAMBOO, INC.**
5 Woods Edge Lane
Houston, TX 77024
(713) 278-7344
(866) 514-3986 toll free
Yucabambu@aol.com

**YUCATÁN BAMBOO, INC.**
Yucatán, Mexico
(997) 971-02-45

**HECHO A MANO (Folk Art Gallery)**
Calle 31, #308
Izamal, Yucatán
(988) 954-03-44

**CERAMICAS MAYAKAT**
Calle 48, #322
Col. Emiliano Zapata Oriente
Mérida, Yucatán
(999) 986-22-03

## SUGGESTED READING

*Mérida Su Gente y Antes de la Fotografía*, 1992
Michel Antochiw, Cultur Servicios
Gobierno del Estado de Yucatán
Instituto Cultura Yucatán

*Modern Maya Houses*, 1938
Robert Wauchope, Carnegie
Institution, Washington, D. C.

*Living Maya*, 1987
Walter F. Morris Jr./Harry N.
Abrams, Inc. Publishers

*Hacienda Tabi, Un Capitulo en la Historia de Yucatán*, 1993
Lourdes Rejón Patrón
Cultur Servicios
Gobierno de Estado de Yucatán

*El Bordado en Yucatán*, 1993
Patricia Etcharren
Casa de las Artesanias
Gobierno del Estado de Yucatán

*The New Hacienda*, 1997
Karen Witynski & Joe P. Carr,
Gibbs Smith, Publisher

*Mexican Details*, 2003
Karen Witynski & Joe P. Carr,
Gibbs Smith, Publisher

A hand-painted tile by Ceramicas Mayakat features Mayan village scenes.